ONE SMILE AT A TIME

ONE SMILE AT A TIME

How An Accidental Do-Gooder Helped Change Millions Of Lives

BRIAN MULLANEY
Co-founder of Smile Train

WITH EVE CLAXTON

NEW YORK

Copyright ©2011 Brian Mullaney
All rights reserved. No part of this book may be used or reproduced in any manner whatsoever without the written permission of the Publisher. Printed in the United States of America.

Library of Congress Cataloging-in-Publication

ISBN:_9781401323929

FIRST EDITION

To my mom,
ROSEMARY,
who taught me never to resist a generous impulse

To my little sister,
MAURA,
who taught me how to live before she died
at the age of 10.

To my wife,
CRICKET,
who makes me a better person every single day.

Never doubt that a small group
of thoughtful, committed people
can change the world.
Indeed, it is the only thing
that ever has.

— MARGARET MEAD

| Foreword | *xiii* |

Part One

Chapter 1: A Tale of Two Cities	23
Chapter 2: Maura	30
Chapter 3: Soccer Boy	45
Chapter 4: Teach a Man to Fish	55
Chapter 5: The Road Map	70
Chapter 6: The Digital Advantage	78
Chapter 7: The Reluctant President	86

Part Two

Chapter 8: A Tale of Two Doctors	102
Chapter 9: Mr. Smile Train India	116
Chapter 10: The Bright Spot	124
Chapter 11: Things They Never Taught Me at Harvard	138
Chapter 12: How to Make a Donor Smile	145
Chapter 13: Christmas in Baghdad	154
Chapter 14: Tracking Smiles	162
Chapter 15: Smile Pinki	172
Chapter 16: Red Flags over Haiti	181

Epilogue	191
Acknowledgements	**197**
Afterword	**209**

.... FOREWORD ....

By Candice Bergen

It all began with my friend Tom Brokaw. Twelve years ago, Tom called me to recommend a new children's charity, called Smile Train. "They are a fantastic group," he explained, "and they have a great idea for helping kids with birth defects who need surgeries all over the world." Tom explained that instead of sending in surgeons from the U.S. into developing countries on medical missions, Smile Train was going to be working with local doctors, training them, funding their work, and really making a difference.

At the time, I knew very little about medical missions or reconstructive surgeries, but helping children was a no-brainer. Soon afterwards I met with Smile Train's co-founder, Brian Mullaney. Brian, a Harvard graduate with a big grin and dazzling social skills, was still working in advertising at the time. A Madison Avenue ad man wasn't my idea of a typical non-profit founder, but Brian's compassion and energy spoke for themselves. At the end of the meeting, I told Brian to keep me posted. If this "teach a man to fish" strategy was truly as innovative and cost-efficient as Brian made it sound, this could indeed change a lot of lives.

At the time of our first meeting, Smile Train was still an idea on a piece of paper: it was going to be an actual train that would travel from town to town, with doctors on board who would help children with birth defects and deformities, while training local doctors to perform this work for their own communities. Things were slow going at first. Every couple of months I would get a note from Brian with a "progress report," which usually had more setbacks than triumphs. I remember the update that explained matter-of-factly how the minister of railways for China had "killed the train idea" but "not to worry, we are charging ahead anyhow!" I had to admit he was dogged and undaunted.

It took almost two years from when we initially met until the first Smile Train surgeries started happening in China in 1999. By now, Smile Train had decided to focus exclusively on working with local doctors to repair cleft lips and palates: birth defects that affect millions of children living in poverty every single day. Children with unrepaired clefts are ostracized in their communities. They're unable to go to school. They suffer needlessly. Meanwhile, a single surgery that takes as little as forty-five minutes can change the life of a child with a cleft forever. Smile Train's work began as a trickle, but soon hundreds of surgeries turned into thousands, and thousands turned into tens of thousands. After covering all of China, Smile Train expanded to India and the rest of Asia and then branched out to South America and Africa.

Before I knew it, it was 2004 and I was sitting in the front row of a Smile Train event in New York celebrating their first hundred thousand surgeries. This event was unlike any charity event that I had ever attended. It wasn't a fundraiser; it was a thank-you event for the donors who had paid for the first hundred thousand surgeries. Smile Train picked up the tab for the entire evening. This was a first. I heard a lot of donors say that no charity had ever invited them to anything for free before. But this was just one more example of the folks who run Smile Train finding ways to do things differently—and better. Instead of dragging everyone out for yet another rubber chicken, they treated us to a night filled with energy and excitement. More than

750 donors gathered from all over the United States, and their passion and enthusiasm for the work of Smile Train was palpable. During the short but intense speeches, you could have heard a pin drop. There were seven standing ovations. Dr. Hirji Adenwalla, one of Smile Train's very best surgeons who had come all the way from India, spoke eloquently about why he has devoted his life to helping the poor.

But by far the best speaker was a tiny fourteen-year-old girl from China. Her name was Wang Li, and she was Smile Train's patient number one. Speaking through an interpreter, Wang Li told us just how difficult her first nine years of life had been. She explained how painful it was to watch her sisters go off to school every day while she was sent out into the field to tend the cattle. She described how she had to wear a scarf over her face whenever she left the house. How she had no friends, no hope, and no future. And how all of that changed the minute she received her surgery. There was not a dry eye in the house.

For seven years, I'd been hearing all these wonderful stories from Brian and his colleagues about how Smile Train was transforming children's lives. But hearing them firsthand from their surgeon and first patient made it sharply personal. I saw that Smile Train really was changing the world, one smile at a time, and I was proud to be on board.

Over the years, I have tried to help in my small way. I send in my donations, of course; I show up at events, I tape and film PSAs, and I joined Smile Train's board of governors. I also visited one of the organization's partner hospitals in Ethiopia and met the surgeons, the parents, and, most importantly, the children. My daughter, Chloe, is also involved. Four years ago she spent the summer in the south of India visiting the same surgeon I had met at the Smile Train celebration in New York.

As Smile Train approaches its one-millionth surgery, the timing of this book's release could not be better. It movingly captures the heartache of parents who have to watch their children suffer because they cannot afford the surgery they need. It celebrates the incredible courage these children demonstrate as they face such difficult lives in the world's poorest countries. It gets inside the minds of these selfless doctors, and shows how a Smile Train surgeon can relieve that suffering in under and hour, giving every child not just a new smile, but a second chance at life.

Reading this book will serve to remind you that it is possible to make a difference, and that there are still are a lot of very good things happening in this world, even if they never make the evening news. And when you are done, you will end up with a smile on your face too. Just like mine.

Candice Bergen,
New York, 2010

ONE SMILE AT A TIME

.... PART ONE ....

BEFORE

.... ONE ....

A Tale of Two Cities

If you met me when I was 29, you probably never would have guessed I'd end up running a children's charity some day.

Back then I was doing my best impersonation of an archetypal yuppie, a Madison Avenue ad man in an Armani suit and Gucci loafers. I had all the accessories: the gold Rolex, the triple black Porsche, the penthouse apartment, and the 5,000-square-foot house in the Hamptons. In 1989, I quit my job as a Senior Vice President at one of the biggest advertising agencies in the world to found my own agency with my business partner, Mike Shell. Our first client was a multi-million dollar computer tech account, and suddenly, we were batting in the big leagues. I was young, single, living the fast life, going to all the parties and nightclubs, eating at the best restaurants. I was making as much money as I could, buying as many things as I could, and having as much fun as I possibly could.

At least that was the way it looked from the outside. On the inside, I knew that I had gotten far too lucky, far too quickly—and as hard as I tried to embrace all the values of upward mobility, there was always some small part of me that knew that at some point, I was going to have to pay some of this good fortune forward.

Blame it on my childhood. I'd been brought up in a middle-class Irish Catholic family who drilled it into me the importance of giving back. My grandmother, Beatrice Hancock Mullaney, was one of the first women to graduate from Boston University Law school in 1927, going on to become the first female probate judge in Massachusetts. She used to tell stories about being a lawyer during the Great Depression, when her clients were so poor they had to pay her with tomatoes and chickens. She was very active in helping others, a devout Catholic, and had a huge influence on my dad. Through a genetic predisposition for hard work inherited from his parents, he rose to Vice Chairman of Gillette where he started a pro bono program for clients who desperately needed legal help, but who couldn't afford to pay. My mother, meanwhile, was one of the most empathetic people I ever met. She was forever raging and rallying against life's inequities, always cheering for the little guy, and those without a voice or a seat at the table. It was my mom who drilled into her five children her favorite saying "Never resist a generous impulse."

Even in the height of my yuppie years, I would hear my mother's soft but stern voice in my head: "never resist, Brian, never resist." Through high school, college and my professional career, I was always looking for ways to give back in whatever way I could. I started volunteering at my church, setting up a computer network for them, bringing them into the 20th century. My ad agency partner Mike Schell and I created a fundraising campaign for a project that worked with young offenders on the Lower East side of Manhattan and for a center for disabilities in Harlem. Still, I was looking for something more substantive. I wanted to be hands on. I'd read an article about Mayor Koch's Office on Volunteerism, so I set up an appointment at City Hall, handing over my application and waiting to be seen by a counselor. An hour later, I told the nice elderly woman behind her desk that I'd like work with young inner city kids, maybe who didn't have a dad or a good home life. Perhaps I could help coach the sports team or volunteer at a Boys Club.

My counselor's nose began to wrinkle.

"What? You want to work with blacks?" she asked. "What a waste! You have a degree from Harvard. How about teaching English to Japanese businessmen? We could use your help doing that."

I was so taken aback that someone would say something like that in New York City in the year 1989, that I told the counselor thank you, but no thank you, and I left. As I walked out the door, the thought went through my head: If I can't find a good charity to help, then maybe I'll have to build one.

It took me a while before I acted on that impulse. Then, some months later, I was sitting on a New York City subway train when I came up with an idea. Every week, I would take the train uptown to see one of my biggest clients, a group of cosmetic surgeons. These surgeons had their offices on Park Avenue, the most glamorous address in New York. Usually, I'd be riding the train in the mid-afternoon, around the time the city schools get out. We'd stop at a station and a hundred public school students would rush on; suddenly the car was overrun with bodies, noise, and commotion. I was going to Park Avenue, the heart of socialite Manhattan. These students were going home to some of the poorest neighborhoods in the city, in the Bronx and Harlem.

Meanwhile, I was on my way to meet with my clients to talk about their latest marketing needs. I'd already created a series of campaigns for them with headlines like: "Look like a million for a couple of thousand!" and "Plastic surgery that doesn't leave you looking plastic!

The campaign had been a runaway success. After one of the ads appeared on TV, the office would get 500 phone calls in a week: so many calls that their phone system would break down from the overload. These were the years of wretched excess in Manhattan when it was all about money, money, money—and cosmetic surgery was becoming the hot thing to do. Wealthy people would pay $15,000 for a face-lift, $5,000 for a nose job, or $10,000 to have liposuction on their thighs. Some clients, we called them "scalpel slaves" would have dozens of procedures.

But these weren't the only operations my surgeons could do. Like most plastic surgeons, in addition to cosmetic work, they could do more essential reconstructive surgeries—correcting birth defects, helping scars to fade, removing lumps and bumps and other marks caused by congenital problems or injuries. Every week, I would ride the subway uptown, and every week, more often than not, I would notice some scrappy kid with some kind of defect or deformity riding right alongside me. I saw children with giant moles and port wine stains on their faces; shiny pink untreated scars from injuries and burns; I even saw crazy deformities such as missing ears or six fingers on one hand (a birth defect my surgeons told me went by the name of hexadactyly). I kept asking myself, how come these kids weren't getting fixed? The inequity was staring me in the face. While I was helping surgeons sell cosmetic surgery to women who often didn't really need it, here were all these inner-city kids who truly needed operations, but weren't being helped. I rode that subway for months, staring at those children—scarred, deformed, neglected—before I decided to do something about it.

I approached the subject gingerly at first. I asked my surgeons if they would be interested in doing free surgeries if I could figure out a program that could identify children from low-income backgrounds who needed their help. The surgeons said yes, probably because they thought I would never follow through. But I did follow through. I thought about handing out business cards on the subway, but that didn't seem like the most legitimate way of approaching things. Instead, I decided to try to go through the public schools. I wrote a letter to the chancellor of the New York City public schools and told him my idea: free reconstructive surgery for inner city kids who couldn't afford it. It sounded simple, but I had no clue how complicated it would get.

I brought my business partner, Mike, on board. The two of us started going to meetings at the Board of Education in Brooklyn. We'd show up and sit there in front of this impenetrable wall of career bureaucrats: an administrator, a principal, an assistant administrator, and a lawyer. The bureaucrats would scratch their heads and say, "The chancellor wants to do this, but we need to know more. For instance, why do you want to do this anyway?" We'd tell them, "Oh, we're just doing it for charity. We're just doing it to do a good thing." But the questions kept coming. "Why do you want to help these kids?" "Why should we give you access to our schools?" "How are you going to make money from this?" So we'd just sit there patiently, answering their questions, telling them we had no intention of making money out of this; that we just wanted to help. We went back to Brooklyn again and again and again, for more than a year.

At the time, I couldn't understand their reasons for stalling. We were offering to arrange free reconstructive surgery for children who needed it, and all we got was the seventh degree! But in hindsight, I can at least appreciate their confusion. To the bureaucrats, Mike and I were just yuppies in the expensive suits. What did we care about helping inner-city kids? Maybe they were hoping that we would give up and go away. But we didn't. We kept going to the meetings. Finally, eighteen months later, we were told that we had the go-ahead for the program and in the months that followed, we rolled it out in seventy-nine public schools in New York City. This was how the program worked: I went and made presentations to the schools, explaining the program. The idea was that a point person at the school—a social worker, guidance counselor, or school nurse—would identify a child who needed help. Then they would invite the parents in for a conference. After the families filled out application forms, the point person at the school would take a Polaroid photo of the child and send it to the ad agency so we could review it and send it onto to our clients the surgeons.

When the pictures started coming in, we couldn't believe our eyes. Terrible scars and birth defects, horrible correctable deformities that had gone untreated for years. What I learned was that these problems were not medical problems; they were economic problems. These kids were from low-income backgrounds. Many of them were from immigrant families who didn't speak English, or whose parents were afraid of being deported, which was why they hadn't taken their son or daughter to a doctor. It was shocking to realize that there were so many children walking around with these problems, and no one cared enough to help them.

Often, the photos that arrived at the ad agency would be heart-breaking. The one that stays in my mind was of an eight-year-old girl whom I'll call Eliza. Her photo arrived with a note from a guidance counselor at her public school in Queens: "Eliza is a small, somewhat shy little girl who is quite brave and who needs your help," the counselor wrote. Eliza had been born with a giant nevus or mole, extending from her right eyebrow, all the way down her cheek below her mouth and across the bridge of her nose. The thing that affected me more than the mole was the look in Eliza's eyes. She looked so ashamed, like would have rather died than have that photo taken. I remember thinking, "If this little girl walked down the hallway of a public school in Greenwich, Connecticut, she would have been tackled and taken to the nearest hospital." But she was from a low-income area of Queens. Her father had died; her mom didn't speak much English, and didn't have the information or means to get Eliza the help she desperately needed. Thankfully, her guidance counselor knew about the program and sent us Eliza's photo.

Right away, we called the top surgeon at Columbia Presbyterian who told us that 100% of these kinds of moles can turn cancerous if they aren't removed. Eliza had been living with her mole for eight years, and it was a time bomb waiting to go off. We rushed her case through. Right away, Eliza underwent a series of tissue expansion and excision procedures to prepare her for surgery. Three months later, she had the operation to remove the mole. Afterwards she came to my office so we could meet her and take photos with her. Eliza had skin grafts on half of her face; even post-operation, the scars were still very much visible. But the giant mole was gone and that look in her eyes had gone altogether. Eliza was smiling and her eyes were sparkling. Over time, she had further scar revision surgeries and she was able to heal. In the end, she looked like any other normal, happy little girl. The transformation was amazing. After a while, it became clear that there was enough demand for the program that we needed to reach out to other plastic surgeons. Soon we had surgeons from of some of the biggest and best hospitals in New York City on board. We started in seventy-nine schools for the pilot program, and then expanded to 500 schools. From there we went to 1,200 city schools; in fact, to every public school in New York City. Hundreds of students were getting help, and they were getting their operations for free. In the end, the entire struggle had been worth it.

I learned a lot from the experience of starting this program in New York City public schools. When you think of the word "charity," you tend to think about the Red Cross or the Salvation Army, big engines with millions of dollars and thousands of staff members at their disposal. But it was really inspiring to know that you could merely have an idea, start small, and really change children's lives. Thanks to the program, I learned that it pays to be audacious: I'd sent a letter to the chancellor of one of the biggest school systems in the United States and he had written me back the next day. I learned that you have to be persistent, that you could conceive of something and then have to fight like crazy to get it off the ground. At the same time, I learned that some things are worth fighting for—there was something very immediate about what we were doing. I could see the results with my own eyes; I met Eliza and others like her; I shook their little hands, and it was thrilling to see that at the end of the day, we'd made a difference. I learned that I could use my entrepreneurial skills in a completely different way: I was building my company and I was building this program at the same time, and there were so many similarities. I had one foot in Park Avenue, the wealthiest place in the world, and another foot in the poorest neighborhoods in New York. What I had proven to myself by starting this program was that in a very simple, very immediate, very concrete way, it was possible to connect the dots.

Twenty years later, I find myself bridging the exact same gap. I'm connecting the dots, helping to figure out the best way to right a wrong by bringing people together. The difference now is that the stakes are no longer local—they're global. Through Smile Train—the children's charity I co-founded in 1999—we're now working with surgeons around the globe to help more than 125,000 children every year in seventy-nine of the poorest countries in the world at the time this book was printed. The numbers have grown exponentially, but the principle remains the same as when I was running the New York City schools program all those years ago: when you remove the obstacles between those who have the talent to help and those who need that help the most, amazing things can happen.

.... TWO ....

Maura

If a therapist wanted to put me on the couch and find out the reason why a yuppie with a Porsche was so determined to get a program for inner-city children off the ground, it probably wouldn't take very long to come up with the answer. In fact, I can probably sum it up in one word: "Maura."

Maura was my little sister. She was this adorable, plump, freckled Irish girl, a real Shirley Temple type: the kind of kid whose dimples showed whenever she smiled. In my memory of her, she smiled all the time. We were a large, close-knit Irish-American family growing up in a middle class suburb of Washington D.C.. My mother had three boys in four years—I was the second in line—and then she had Maura, the daughter she'd always longed for. I was three years older than Maura, but we were the best of friends.

Maura was eight years old when she got sick. I was in junior high in seventh grade. The school coach came and found me and said, "You have to go home right away." My Dad was working in the White House and unreachable, my Mom was in a panic and called the school to send me home. My sister had a fever of 107. She was convulsing, having delusions.

We wrapped her up, brought her to the car, and raced to the hospital. Maura almost died that day. The doctors had no idea what was wrong with her. It was only later that we learned that she had a rare syndrome called Stevens-Johnson. Her immune system was under attack. Her fever had gone so high that it had fried her internal organs. Her temperature actually bubbled the skin off her frame. She had horrible, painful lesions everywhere, even on her tongue and in her eyes. Within weeks, her young body shriveled into a 90-year old shell. Maura was half blind. She couldn't walk. She was eight years old, and she was being pushed around in a wheelchair wearing big, dark glasses because her pupils were burned from the fever. She went from 70 pounds down to 40 pounds. All her hair was gone. She was in constant pain. Day-to-day existence was a continual, agonizing struggle. But despite the way that she looked, and the acute degree of her pain, she actually had the courage to go back to school. Maura didn't want to be bedridden and confined to the house. She wanted to be out in the world. What did she get for her bravery? At school she was tormented and teased and ruined. It was terrible. The other kids didn't understand. They had no sympathy for this little girl who didn't fit in. All they saw was a monster. My brothers and I had the job of pushing Maura around in her wheelchair. People stared at her wherever she went, and we glowered back, daring them to say something. But nothing we could do was going to stop the pointing and the looks. During the time of Maura's illness, I experienced in a very direct way what it means to be ostracized because of the way you look to others. It was an experience I have never forgotten.

At a certain point it became clear that Maura was going to die. I remember— vividly— watching a Miss America pageant with her on TV one evening. Maura was staring at all these beautiful women, talking about what they wanted to do in the future, and meanwhile she couldn't even look in the mirror. She knew that she would never grow up, never fall in love, or get married. Never have a career or a baby. She had no future at all.

My parents did everything they could to save her, they flew all over the country, they brought her to all the top hospitals and specialists. But two years later, Maura died at the age of 10. None of us were ever the same. My parents all but fell apart. Since then, I've learned that the vast majority of couples who go through the experience of losing a child get divorced because it's just too traumatic. My mother and father stuck it out together, in large part because of my little brother, who was a year old when my sister got sick. But they never fully recovered. When my sister died, my mom stopped going to church. My dad retreated into his work. We seldom heard Maura's name around the house. We just didn't talk about her. The first time the name "Maura" was used again on a regular basis in our family was when my wife had the brilliant idea of giving our own baby daughter my sister's beautiful name.

I was 13 when my sister died—a formative age—and her death had a profound effect on me. I developed a real sense of despising things that are unfair—of inequity—because what had happened to Maura never should happen to anyone. It gave me a huge amount of empathy for people who are dealt a bad hand in life. I knew how powerless you can feel when tragedy strikes out of nowhere. My parents did everything they could, but even so, they still had to sit there and watch their daughter suffer so terribly and eventually die.

Because of what happened to Maura, I learned that there are no guarantees. From a very young age I understood that you really have to live and appreciate every day because it can all be gone in the blink of an eye. The experience of Maura's illness and death gave me a real sense of urgency. After she died, I wanted to hit everything full speed. Even at 13 years old, I knew that the biggest tragedy is to die without ever having lived. People talk about having a bucket list; how you're supposed to wait until you're 60 to write it. Well, I started mine when I was 13 years old. At 16, I was skydiving out of an airplane. At 18, I rode a motorcycle cross-country. I did a lot of crazy things—some of them that I probably shouldn't have been doing—but I was determined to extract every ounce out of every experience that life had to offer me.

When I was a senior in high school, I decided I wanted to go to Harvard, my father's alma mater. This was by far the most difficult, long-shot college choice I could have made. I was a good student, but no genius. I was unsure, but my mother egged me on. "Set your mind to it and you can do it," she told me. I had in my favor that

I'd received a fantastic education at The Belmont Hill School in Massachusetts, and that I was considered "well-rounded." I was an all-star in football and co-captain of the track team. I wrote letters to the football coach at Harvard, to the track coach, to the admissions director. I got on their radar and I got in.

My first semester was miserable. My freshman class was made up of perfect National Merit Scholar students with impeccable SAT scores, and I felt like I just didn't fit in. I'd set my heart on playing football, but then, four weeks after joining the freshman football team, one of the trainers noticed something wrong with my neck. A few X-rays later, I learned I'd actually broken it during a high school game, and that the injury had gone undiagnosed. I had a big bone spur in one of my vertebrae and a chip in another. The surgeon told me I was one tackle away from a wheelchair and that I was lucky I wasn't already paralyzed. This was the good news. The bad news was that I had to stop playing football. I came home for Thanksgiving dejected and depressed, and announced to my family I wasn't going back to Harvard. My poor parents had just gotten done putting Harvard stickers on the cars. The discussions that ensued were not pretty and it quickly became clear I needed to get as far away from the situation as possible. I sold my stereo and bought a one way airplane ticket to Los Angeles. I'd never been to California. I didn't know anyone out there, but what I did know was that it was a very long way away from Boston. My parents thought I had lost my mind. My dad drove me to the airport. Right before I got on the plane he said he wanted to give me something. Thank God, I thought. He's going to give me some money help me get started. Instead my father took off his London Fog raincoat and handed it to me. We hugged. As soon as he walked away, I looked in raincoat pockets to see if there was a check inside, but the pockets were empty.

Not giving me a hand-out that day was one of the best things my father ever did for me. In the next year, I grew up a lot. I took a job as a bank teller in Beverly Hills making $636 a month. I found a furnished apartment in a seedy section of Hollywood. I bought a used motorcycle so I could get to work. After paying for the deposit on my apartment and the bike, I had about $50 left to get me through my first two weeks and my first paycheck. I calculated that even after I started earning, I was going to have six dollars a day for food and gas. I was so broke I had to think carefully before ordering at McDonald's. There's a song called, "It Never rains in Southern California" but when I arrived there in January of 1978 it rained almost every day. I remember driving my motorcycle drenched, wearing my dad's London Fog raincoat, going to work at a bank in Beverly Hills, cashing checks for some of the wealthiest people in America, while I was living on six dollars a day. This was an education that even Harvard could not give me.

Worst of all, I was incredibly lonely. I was 18 years old in a town where I had no family or friends. I tried crashing parties at UCLA and USC, but it was difficult. No one could understand why I wasn't in college and why I was a bank teller. Without a social life, I had a lot of time on my hands, so when I came across an ad in the LA Times for crisis telephone counselors at The Suicide Prevention Center of Los Angeles, I called them up and interviewed as a volunteer. I became the youngest counselor they'd ever had. One night a week from ten o'clock at night until four o'clock in the morning, I would handle calls on the suicide hotline. The phones were busy all evening—I would finish a call and within five seconds, the phone would ring again. Part of our job was to vet the caller and if we thought it was serious we would send the police and paramedics. I remember listening on the other end of the phone as the police broke down the door of a woman's kitchen after she passed out from an overdose. I remember talking a kid down off a roof of a building. I also remember getting a follow-up report about a young guy who had been sexually abused by his uncle and who had tried kill himself immediately after hanging up with me. It was heavy stuff for an 18 year old, but I learned a lot what happens to people at their most desperate moments in life, and what it means to truly listen.

After only a few months in Los Angeles, I realized with absolute clarity that I needed to get myself back to college. I wrote letters to Harvard. I begged. I pleaded, and the following academic year, I managed to start back there again. I'd had enough of a taste of the real-world now—working 50 weeks out of the year just to pay the bills—that this time, I appreciated every single moment of college and took nothing for granted. I majored in business and economics. I started my own student-run advertising agency while still at Harvard. I was wandering around campus one day when I started thinking about all the bulletin boards and lampposts on campus, all of them covered with fliers. The thought went through my head, "fliers are basically advertisements." If I could make a flier look nice, I could call it an advertisement and charge $50 for it. There were hundreds of flyers all over the campus so I did the math and realized I could probably make a lot of money. I had business cards made. I learned to typeset. I started putting on a suit, renting a car, and driving around to local businesses, drumming up accounts. No one knew I was a student, or if they guessed, they didn't let on. I wrote the headlines, designed ads, made the posters, and created the logos. My "agency" grossed more than $100,000 in revenues the first year.

When I graduated from Harvard in 1983, I went straight to Madison Avenue. I took a job at Young and Rubicam advertising agency as a junior copywriter, writing box-top copy for Jello on a salary of $15,000, a serious pay-cut from my college job. I never was a very good writer—I was an economics guy—but ultimately this worked to my advantage. All the copywriters that I met were frustrated novelists. Meanwhile, I'd figured out that advertising is all about ideas, and even if I wasn't the greatest writer, I could be good with ideas. Slowly but surely I worked my way up the ladder. I moved to another agency, until I ended up the Senior Vice President and Creative Director at J. Walter Thompson at the age of 28.

I was happy in my job, but even so, I knew that I was an entrepreneur at heart, and that I wanted to chart my own course. Everyone said I was crazy to quit my job. I was doing so well; walking away was too much of a risk. But it was like skydiving out of a plane all over again. I couldn't resist. I took my life savings and started an ad agency out of my apartment. I would put a suit on every day and go to work in my kitchen. Those early days were scary, but I knew there had to be more life than being a cog in a wheel at a corporation.

Maura didn't get a chance at life, but I was determined to never settle.

After the business took off, I felt a real urgency to do something to give back. I might never have vocalized it at the time, but when I started the program with the city's public schools, the program had everything to do with Maura and what I had learned from pushing her around in her wheelchair—that for a child who has some kind of deformity, the taunts and the glares are the worst part of all. As my parents tried, there was nothing anyone could do to help Maura. But when it came to these school children, their problems were correctable. We could help them. We started the program, and it was working. These kids were getting the surgeries they needed, and that was amazing to me. It was becoming addictive. The more surgeries I helped to arranged, the more children I wanted to help.

We called the program "Operation Smile" because that was the goal: making children smile thanks to surgery. It got off to a fast start and was helping hundreds of children in no time. We were thinking about how to expand it nationally when one day, I was sitting at my desk at my office on Madison Avenue in New York when I stumbled upon something that changed my course all over again. It was lunchtime; I was eating a sandwich and leafing through People magazine. I turned the page; suddenly, the words "Operation Smile" leapt out at me. I started to read. It turned out there was another plastic reconstructive surgery initiative helping children, also called Operation Smile! How did that happen?

I read the rest of the article. As it turned out, our Operation Smile and the other one were quite different. Ours was completely focused on helping children in New York City; the other was a volunteer mission group operating on children all over the world. This other organization was also much better established than we were: it had been founded ten years previously by a plastic surgeon called Dr. Bill Magee and his wife Kathy, a former nurse and social worker.

Right away, I saw the potential. What if there was some way for our two organizations to collaborate? Without hesitating, I fired off a very friendly letter to Bill and Kathy, introducing myself and asking for a meeting. Soon after that I got a call from Bill suggesting that we get together. So I jumped on a plane and went down to the Operation Smile headquarters in Norfolk, Virginia. Although the organization's offices were pretty modest in scale—housed in a warehouse in a rundown part of town—it was obvious that amazing things were happening here. Everywhere I looked, there were boxes and crates waiting to be packed with medical supplies to be taken on missions. There were big chalkboards, scrawled with the names of exotic destinations, dates, team rosters, and the names of mission coordinators. The staff members were young, just out of college and wet behind the ears, but bursting with enthusiasm and passion.

The Magees were obviously a big deal. On the walls were framed photos of them receiving all kinds of awards and accolades. There was a letter of recommendation from Mother Teresa. There were photos of them with Ronald Reagan and George and Barbara Bush, and award statues, medals, and articles in every direction. Spending time at the organization's headquarters was instantly humbling. That day, I learned that while I was trying to reach a few hundred schoolchildren in New York City, there were millions of children all over the developing world who desperately needed reconstructive plastic surgeries. That day I saw pictures of children with horrific birthmarks and defects, terrible sores brought on by malnutrition and infection; awful, raw, untreated burns; shocking traumatic injuries. The people at Operation Smile described for me the wretched conditions of children living in refugee camps, in remote villages, in some of the poorest corners of the planet. They explained to me that in developing countries, families have to pay for most medical care, and because of this, the least fortunate members of the population have zero access to basic health provisions, let alone surgery. When you make a dollar a day, an expensive surgery is out of the question. These parents could save every spare penny their whole lives, and never have enough to get a child the operation he or she desperately needs.

So many of the health problems created and exacerbated by poverty feel insurmountable, but reconstructive surgery was one thing that was a guaranteed fix. Unlike malaria, most surgical problems don't come back. You just had to get the right surgeon to the right place, and everything else would follow. It wasn't as if you had to wait to find the cure; the cure existed. All that was needed was enough money and the will to make it happen. With the schools program, I'd been putting two and two together. This organization was doing the same thing, only on a much, much larger scale, and in places where it was clear that the level of hardship was like nothing I'd ever known.

Right away, I saw a niche for myself. Bill was a plastic surgeon. Kathy was a social worker. From what I could see, marketing wasn't their strong suit. This would be a natural way for me to contribute to their organization. I knew I could help with fundraising too. Later that same year, we made the decision to fold our Operation Smile into theirs. I joined their board of directors. The idea was that I would work on taking my schools program nationwide, while helping to raise money and awareness for overseas missions at the same time.

Right away, I began planning to go along on one of the medical missions so I could see the organization's work with my own eyes. Throughout my career I'd always been fanatical about doing major research. When I was fresh out of college, a junior copywriter trainee, I worked on every brand imaginable. I traveled everywhere—to factories, focus groups, stores, conventions, trade shows, sales meetings, farms, paper mills, shopping malls— trying to learn everything I could about every product I ever tried to sell. I learned why some potato chips have green spots (because the potato was exposed to sunlight while it was growing, releasing chlorophyll); why one kind of beer is darker than another (because the lighter beer uses rice in addition to hops and barley malt); and what the inside of a nuclear power plant looks like (pretty scary, especially when you are standing next to the tank that holds the twelve-foot-long spent fuel rods). I had always believed that the more I expanded my experience of the product, the better qualified I was going to be able to describe it and communicate what was so great about it to consumers. It followed that if I was going to try to raise awareness and money for this charity, then I had to understand how it worked from the ground up.

There was going to be a mission to China in a couple of months, and I told the Magees I wanted to go along. This was how I ended up making my first trip to Asia—to Guangdong province on the southern coast of China. Our mission began with a marathon journey. We flew from New York to Los Angeles and from Los Angeles to Hong Kong, descending into the city via the old Kai Tak airport; the plane taking us so low over the rooftops that we could see inside people's living rooms. When we stepped off the plane, limbs aching from being cramped in a cabin for twenty hours, the heat and humidity hit us like a wall of steam. Our final destination was a small hospital in a remote village in the most populated province in China. Now that the twenty-hour flight was over, we boarded the subway, and then took a train to the Chinese border, where we were loaded into a van, all of us bleary-eyed from the journey. My travel companions were the Magees and DeLois Greenwood, who was their right-hand woman. DeLois had started out as a volunteer scrub nurse on the missions, but since then had made herself indispensable to everyone, she wore a million hats, organizing the missions, raising money, and generally keeping everyone on track. I liked DeLois immediately—and she remains one of the most impressive and selfless people I have ever met.

In our little van, we shot past the newly developed industrial area of Shenzhen. I was desperately trying to grab a bit of sleep along the way, but soon enough, the good road ran out and I was jerked awake, the driver swerving to avoid a gruesome car accident. An eight-hour, bone-jarring ride later, we arrived at the hostel where we were staying and were taken to a restaurant to eat. I forced some food down before collapsing into bed at 4 A.M. Two hours later I forced myself awake again. By 6:30 A.M. we pulled up at the hospital to begin the day of surgeries.

Walking up to this large, drab, gray building, it was hard to believe that this actually was a medical establishment; it looked more like a prison. We picked our way over crumbling concrete steps into a dark hallway lit by a single bare light bulb. It occurred to me that even the worst medical institution in the whole United States would look like a five-star establishment compared to this place. The advance team had arrived a few days before us, so surgery could begin as soon as Magee walked in the door and scrubbed up. Two tables were awaiting him, enabling him to operate on one child while the other one was being prepped. Meanwhile, crowds of patients were already beginning to gather. The lines stretched through the hospital and out the door. I began walking up and down, shaking hands and introducing myself via our interpreter. I wanted to conduct interviews and shoot video that we could later use in promotional materials.

This was my introduction to the world of people who live at the very bottom of the economic pyramid. The people who'd brought their children here to be helped were peasants, rice farmers, earning daily wages, the tiniest pittance on which to keep their families alive. Dirt was ingrained in their faces, in the lines on their palms, and in the frayed edges of their clothing. When we shook hands, I could feel that their skin was as calloused and rough as sandpaper. I guessed that most of them must be younger than I was, even though they looked much older. Like their parents, the children were grimy and dressed in rags, but it was the sheer numbers and the severity of the deformities that made my heart stop. Here were children with untreated burns. Babies with giant tumors on their cheeks and foreheads. Eight- and nine-year-olds with clubfeet. Little girls and boys with terrible birthmarks and defects marring their faces. The children were so young that they were oblivious to what was happening, but the parents were jittery with anxiety. It was awful to see the combination of hope and fear in the expressions on these parents' faces.

I began asking my questions. Why are you here? How did you get here? Every parent gave me more or less the same answer: "I'm a peasant. I never thought I could be able to help my child in this way." I learned that people had traveled for hundreds of kilometers to get to the hospital because they heard that surgeries were being offered free of charge. More and more people kept coming. I couldn't get over the numbers.

In New York, I'd received one or two envelopes a week with photos of children who needed surgery. Here I was faced with over 200 children in a single day, each with at least one parent in tow, and all of those parents waiting with the same tense, desperate look in their eyes.

I couldn't take it all in. I realized that I needed to focus on one child; a single individual to make sense of this. One little girl stood out to me. I asked the doctors and her father if it would be okay if I followed her so I could take some photos and go into surgery with her. Maybe I could even try to put her at ease. Her name was Li Yin Kan, which someone told me roughly translated meant "Colorful Cloud." She was nine years old. Her hair was cut in a little bob with bangs above her eyebrows and she was very pretty, from the nose up. But the area between Colorful Cloud's mouth and her nose was horribly twisted and malformed. She had a big gap in her upper lip below her right nostril, extending into her gum. Her front teeth had grown at odd angles, making her look even more monstrous. Colorful Cloud had what is called a cleft lip.

Before volunteering on a surgical mission, I had never seen a cleft lip before. By now I knew that clefts are one of the world's most common birth defects. In a normal foetus, the baby's head grows around the spinal column from both sides, fusing in the middle of the upper lip. But for cleft children, the fusing fails to happen completely. No one knows exactly why this happens—there's a genetic strain involved, but environmental and nutritional factors may also have an influence. What we do know is that a simple surgery can fix this defect a few months after the baby is born. One in seven hundred babies are born with clefts in both the U.S. (one in 500 births in China,) but in the U.S., every cleft is fixed within the first three month's of a baby's life, leaving nothing behind but a small scar. Meanwhile, in developing countries, families aren't so lucky. In places like China, where many families have to pay for medical care, the vast majority of babies born with clefts never receive surgery at all because it's too expensive. Meanwhile, local hospitals often have limited staff and facilities, and surgeons who might want to treat underprivileged patients are held back by lack of resources. In countries where medical provision is scarce, as you can imagine, repairing a birth defect like this one falls very low on the list of priorities—in fact, in China, clefts don't even make the official list of disabilities. They're seen as a cosmetic problem: "not life threatening."

Yet the life of a child with a cleft isn't much of a life at all. In most cultures, the children born with these defects are considered cursed by God. They're treated like outcasts in their communities, taunted and teased, unable to go to school. Clefts are particularly hard on young girls like Colorful Cloud, whose value is often measured by their looks. These girls may never marry or be able to have a job, which means they will remain an economic burden on their parents throughout their lives. The ripples of misery are far-reaching, not just for the child, but also for the whole family. Even siblings find themselves shunned, and the child with the cleft is often accused of bringing a curse on the entire village. Because people don't tend to know what causes the defect, superstitions run rife: the family made a pact with the devil, the mother held a knife during an eclipse, the wife was unfaithful to her husband. For many impoverished parents, a cleft is one more problem than they can bear. I'd heard stories of children with clefts being abandoned, given away to orphanages, or left by the roadside to die. One doctor told me he came across a very young boy with a severe cleft who was tied to a tree for years because his family thought he was a dog. So much horror caused by a simple birth defect that could be repaired by surgery.

As we waited to prep Colorful Cloud for her operation, I tried to get to know this little girl and her father better. With the help of an interpreter and by using hand gestures and smiles, we managed to get along pretty well. I found out that Colorful Cloud had parents who loved her and cared about her, that her father had brought her here today, traveling over 200 km from their home to the hospital by bus and on foot. I learned that this man was a rice farmer, desperately poor. The cost of the surgery would have exceeded his annual income and as a result, his daughter had suffered with her cleft for nearly ten years. Colorful Cloud had never been to school. Instead, she spent her days at home, in virtual hiding. No wonder this father had spent everything he had to get here—free surgery was his only hope of giving his daughter a future in life. When I looked at Colorful Cloud, I felt such a pang for her. Many defects can be concealed, but not this one. Her cleft was right in the middle of her face. For her entire life, there had been no way of escaping from it. At least not until now.

When it came time for this little girl to say good-bye to her father, she was trembling and he looked just as terrified. It was my job to carry Colorful Cloud into the OR while her father waited outside. I put her gently on the table. Machines were beeping all around us. I held her hand, while doing my best to smile at her so as to let her know that everything was going to be just fine. Then I handed her the anesthesia mask and showed her how to hold it up to her face. Colorful Cloud put the mask to her face, fell back, and within a minute, she was fast asleep.

Bill got ready to start the operation. He began by sketching the procedure, marking the areas of her lips and skin where he wanted to cut. Then he made a large incision in the lip, explaining that he was going to undo her lip so that he could piece it back together again. He handed me a pair of clamps and said, "Here, hold this." Suddenly I was responsible for holding up the flap of lip while Bill worked on separating further pieces of her upper lip and nose—areas of her face that had bonded, or failed to bond, in all the wrong places. I'm someone who is queasy at the best of times; I hate the sight of blood. Meanwhile, it was 100 degrees, I had scrubs on over my clothing, and I was drenched with sweat, functioning on less the four hours' sleep in the past 36 hours. A wave of nausea came over me. I started to sway and felt my knees buckle beneath me. I quickly handed the clamp to the nearest nurse and left the room to recover. Wholly embarrassed and still queasy, I put my head between my legs and waited. Fifteen minutes later I took a deep breath, stood up, and went back in. I returned just in time to see Bill slowly and carefully sewing the pieces of Colorful Cloud's lip back together. He was lifting up each flap, realigning it, then sewing it into its new position, stitching deftly and quickly from the base of the nose all the way down, as if he was assembling the pieces in a jigsaw.

Back in the operating room, I was careful to keep my eyes on the clock. I'd been told that cleft surgery takes approximately 45 minutes. Could something so seemingly complicated be accomplished that quickly? Exactly 30 minutes later, the surgery was complete. With the use of sutures, a scalpel, and a surgeon's expert hands, the entire operation was over in about 45 minutes.

I picked up Colorful Cloud, limp in my arms, so I could carry her back to her father in the waiting room. Her lip was swollen, and there was a row of tiny stitches from all the way up to her nose. Even so, she was unrecognizable from the little girl I'd carried into the OR less than an hour ago. Her father lifted Colorful Cloud out of my arms, staring at his own daughter in amazement, as if he was seeing her for the first time. Was this the same little girl he had handed to me less than an hour ago? Colorful Cloud had a fat lip, but it would soon heal. Meanwhile, the horrifying cleft was gone. Despite the stitches and swelling, Colorful Cloud was already living up to her beautiful name.

I couldn't wait for Colorful Cloud to wake up and see the transformation. Her father lay her down on a bed and we sat together, waiting, both of us holding her hands.

Twenty minutes later, she woke up. She was still groggy, but she was starting to look around. I was on the edge of my seat. The nurse brought her a mirror and handed it to Colorful Cloud. She hesitated, then slowly held the mirror up to her face. I expected her to laugh, gasp, or shout with joy at the sight of her new smile. Instead, she said nothing. She just stared at her reflection.

I began to think that something was wrong. Was she unhappy with the way she looked?

Her father let out a sob, sucking in his breath to try and hold back his emotion. By now, I was in tears. I couldn't help myself; it's impossible to be in the room after a surgery like this and not be deeply moved.

I came away from the OR that day convinced that I had just witnessed a medical miracle. Now that her lip was fixed, Colorful Cloud would be able to go to school. She would be able to work, and maybe even marry some day. Her life had been changed forever; so had her father's life, and her mother's. I thought of my own parents. They had searched everywhere for a miracle for my sister Maura, but there was nothing anyone could do: Maura had a problem that was incurable, that could never be fixed. That day with Colorful Cloud, I'd seen firsthand how a stunningly simple, inexpensive procedure could so utterly transform a child's world. This was a problem that could absolutely be fixed, and the results were dramatic, immediate, significant, and lasting.

Just as Colorful Cloud was transformed that day, so was I.

.... THREE ....

Soccer Boy

My next mission started with a bang and ended with a whimper.

It was November 1995, and I found myself standing in front of dozens of Vietnamese reporters and photographers, at a press conference in Hanoi, announcing our mission's arrival in Vietnam. There were five of us going up in front of the cameras: Bill Magee, myself, and three others from the organization. I had a microphone with my name card on it. I was 34 and participating in my first press conference. I remember squinting as the flash bulbs went off and thinking, "wow!"

"Ladies and Gentleman," Magee began. "Thank you from the bottom of our hearts for this incredible welcome today! We are honored and moved. Twenty years ago, our two nations were still at war. Now, the American people have sent us here in the spirit of peace and reconciliation. We are a group of forty-nine American volunteers—including doctors, nurses, surgeons, pediatricians—all here on a mission… to bring free reconstructive surgery to Vietnamese children!"

There was a round of applause. In 1995, the U.S. trade embargo, which had been in place since the end of the war, had been lifted only the year before. Only a few months earlier, diplomatic relations between the U.S. and Vietnam had been restored. As a result, the arrival of an American mission made up of doctors and surgeons to help Vietnamese children was front-page news.

"Why would you come here?", one of the reporters wanted to know.

"Years ago we were fighting each other," Magee said, "Now we're here to work together, to change the lives of children with birth defects and other deformities, and at no cost to their families or to your government."

Another round of applause.

It was a fascinating time to be in Vietnam. Everywhere we went in Hanoi, there were signs of growth and industry. Buildings were going up. Foundations were being dug. New shops and restaurants were opening. The Vietnamese government had instituted economic reforms, and there was a tremendous energy in the air; a feeling that things were going to get better, that progress was possible. This was a country that had been decimated by the war and by the U.S. embargo. And here we were, a group of wealthy Americans, announcing that we were here to save the children. I felt pretty pleased with myself. I smiled, held my thumbs up, and had my photo taken. It was pretty thrilling.

The next day our picture appeared in all the papers: "American Mission Group Arrives to Help Vietnamese Children." When we went to meet with the Minister of Commerce at Hanoi's equivalent of Capitol Hill, again, photos were staged. I had my name on another microphone. Later that day, we met with our local donors, who included some major bankers and business people. Everyone kept referring to the mission and the ground-breaking work we were doing to help forge new U.S.-Vietnamese relations. I began to feel as if I was helping head up a U.N. delegation.

By the time we boarded our bus to leave Hanoi, I was feeling very pleased with our reception, and by how well we were being received. Now we were heading north, toward the province of Bac Thai and the small city of Thai Nguyen, where we were going to be operating on children who would never be able to afford reconstructive surgery without our help. The last time Americans were here, they were 20,000 feet in the air, dropping bombs. This time we were coming with medical supplies, bringing hope to the children.

The further we traveled, the more rutted and dusty the roads became, and the more primitive the architecture. The substantial dwellings of the capital city were soon behind us, replaced by lean-tos, roofing made of tin or shaded with palm fronds. All along the roadside, we passed paddy fields, palm trees and water buffaloes. People carried their wares on their heads and the backs of bicycles. I grew up seeing films like The Deerhunter and Apocalypse Now. I couldn't believe I was traveling through this landscape that was so familiar to me from the movies.

Outside the bus windows, there was something else that stood out to me: cemetery after cemetery, rows upon rows of white crosses. I asked our guide about the tombstones. What were they exactly?

"They're anonymous graves," he told me.

The bus rumbled on. After every bend in the road we came upon another cemetery. "Why so many cemeteries?" I asked this time. Of course, the moment the question left my mouth, I regretted it.

"This war touched every family, every person," the guide told me patiently. "More than 5 million Vietnamese died out of a population of 40 million. This means we have many graves."

I was stunned. I knew that there were over 58,000 names on the Vietnam Memorial wall in Washington D.C. because I'd seen them with my own eyes. But 5 million Vietnamese? I sat staring out of the window, trying to figure out what that meant in a country of this size. I also started wondering how we were going to be received at our destination, in a country where we were responsible for so much loss, so much suffering. Hanoi was the capitol city. It was cosmopolitan. They were probably used to American visitors. But I had no way of knowing what to expect from people living in a rural area like Bac Thai. Would they shout at us? Tell us to go home? Throw rocks at us? For the rest of the journey, I pretty much held my breath.

Three hours later, we stepped off our bus to a reception unlike anything else we'd ever experienced.

The people of Thai Nguyen didn't shout. They didn't throw rocks. No one said a word. They stood and stared at us with their jaws on the ground, everyone with the same look of shock and bemusement on their faces. Stepping off that bus, I felt like an alien who had fallen from the sky. Later, our guide explained to us the reaction: For most people living in Thai Nguyen, this was the first time they had ever seen Caucasian faces. Although the U.S. army had bombed this city by air, American soldiers had never made it to the ground. No wonder the citizens looked surprised. But once the people of Thai Nguyen got over their initial amazement, we were greeted with smiles and the same word repeated over and over—"Hello, hello, hello!"—wherever we went. Despite everything that had happened between our two nations, these people were waving to us and greeting us, using the one English word that everyone seemed to know.

As it turned out, this "city" was little more than a village, a collection of dusty roadways and reed and bamboo huts. There were no other motorized vehicles in sight, just people going by on foot or on bicycles. As we peered into the darkness of the dwellings, we could see people cooking on open fires, on dirt floors. Our guide explained that Thai Nguyen was impoverished even by Vietnamese standards. The average per capita income at that time was $150, which comes out at 42 cents per day. Electricity was in short supply. Running water was limited and working toilets, an absolute luxury. Even so, there was that same sense of activity and hubbub we'd encountered in Hanoi. People were banging hammers, digging with shovels, carrying goods to market on the backs of their bicycles. The most bizarre sight of all was people still wearing the old Viet Cong helmets, using them as sun hats to shield their eyes from the glare of the sun.

The night of our arrival, the advance team of volunteers filled us in on everything that had been going on while we'd been mugging for the cameras in Hanoi. For the past four days, they'd been screening the patients, and it had been an epic task. More than 400 kids showed up: children with terrible burns, clefts, clubfeet, tumors, every kind of defect imaginable. The crowds were still swarming outside the hospital. At the end of the fourth day, the names of the lucky were scrawled on a blackboard.

The families crowded around, desperate to find out who had made the list. There were around 140 names posted. There wasn't the time, money, or resources to do any more than this.

Over two hundred families had to be turned away. While we'd been smiling and applauding ourselves in Hanoi, volunteers were having to tell families "Sorry, there's no room." I tried to imagine what it felt like to sit down and explain to a mother who has walked for six days with a baby on her back in the hope of receiving surgery: "We'll try to get back here next year." At this point, you wouldn't need an interpreter; the mother's tears and her pleas would tell you everything you needed to know. I didn't think I could do what these brave advance team volunteers were having to do, comforting these families as best they could. It was absolutely heartbreaking for everyone.

The next day, we made straight for the hospital. Three makeshift operating rooms were set up with 10,000 pounds of top-of-the-line medical supplies and equipment shipped all the way from the U.S. In comparison to the operating room, which had a single rickety gurney for an operating table and paint peeling from the walls, our American equipment practically gleamed. The hospital staff members were obviously used to working in compromised circumstances, because their eyes widened at the sight of so much shiny, brand new stuff.

While the surgeons performed their surgeries, I roamed around the hospital, taking pictures, interviewing people, asking them to tell me their stories: how far they'd come, what life was like for them. More often than not, I found myself spending time with the children waiting for their surgeries, as I'd done with Colorful Cloud in China. Unlike with the adults, the language barrier was never a problem with kids. I could always communicate through smiles, hand-gestures, and most importantly, the international language of goofing around, perhaps the greatest skill I brought along with me on this mission.

The hospital was built around a large courtyard, and most afternoons, I'd wander out there to get some air and see who was around. One afternoon, I met a little boy, about nine years old, standing alone in a corner of the courtyard. He had an old basketball under his arm, and as there wasn't a hoop in sight, so I gestured to him to see if he'd like to kick it around. Like Colorful Cloud, he had a severe cleft lip. When he opened his mouth to speak or smile, I could see that he also had a cleft palate, which meant that his defect affected the roof of his mouth, splitting it into two complete parts. And yet despite the gap in his lip where his front teeth protruded from the bottom of his nose, and the deep groove in the roof of his mouth making it difficult for him to speak, his smile was brilliant and he used it often. The cleft and the smile were such an unlikely combination that I was immediately drawn to him. Before I knew it, we were playing soccer together every afternoon.

Our local interpreter and the doctors and nurses kept telling me his name, but I've never been very good at languages. I tried, but I couldn't pronounce it, and now, all these years later, it's slipped from my memory altogether. Back then, I gave him the nickname "Soccer Boy." We became fast friends.

Soccer Boy was one of those kids who seemed to be in a permanent good mood. All week, he kept me entertained, stealing the ball, laughing, and weaving in between the legs of the other volunteers, these giant Americans who soon gathered around to play ball with him. Soccer Boy's high spirits were an inspiration to me. This was a child who had every reason to feel downhearted. It was hard for him to speak. He wasn't able to go to school. He was ridiculed and rejected wherever he went. And yet he was always smiling, always happy to see me.

I never found out how far he'd come to get to the hospital. I never met his parents. But someone loved him, because they had recently given him a haircut—he had these short, jagged bangs above his eyes—and in contrast to the severity of his cleft, the skin on the rest of his face was smooth and unmarked. His eyes were bright and mischievous. He was a skinny little kid, probably suffering from malnutrition, but even so, he was fast and energetic. I felt an enormous relief and sense of gratification that his life was going to change after his surgery. Maybe he would grow up and become a great soccer player some day. Maybe he'd score the winning goal for Vietnam in the World Cup. I kept imagining that his future after his operation was going to be just as bright as his smile.

As the days went on, I became so involved in the world of the hospital and the people I was meeting here, that my everyday life in New York began to seem like a very distant memory. Then I got a harsh reminder. Midway through the trip, I returned to our hostel to find an emergency message waiting. It was scrawled in broken English on a torn piece of paper. "Emergency, call Patricia from New York right away."

This was weird. Patricia was one of my clients at my ad agency. Why would she be calling me in Vietnam?

There was an old wooden phone booth in the hostel, and I managed to get an AT&T operator on the line.

When Patricia answered, she sounded relieved.

"Thank God I finally reached you," she said. "We need some new ads for our corporate image campaign. We want to launch in two months—think you can get me something by Friday?"

I was speechless. This was the emergency? I wished she could see where I was right now. The facilities in the hostel were positively medieval: rats crawling out of the toilet, dirt floors, this broken down old phone booth. It was a miracle that I'd even got a line out of here. The idea that I could just sit down and sketch up some ads for her was completely laughable!

I took a deep breath before I responded. Rule number one of running an ad agency: don't shout at the clients.

I explained to Patricia that I was in a very remote area of Vietnam, volunteering on a medical mission, and that I couldn't really drop everything and create a bunch of new ads explaining why her multi-billion dollar corporation was so wonderful, incredible, and special. This client happened to work at one of the richest corporations on earth. In my head, I was already calculating how many surgeries we could buy with the proceeds of their annual ad budget alone. If they would just throw some extra millions our way, we wouldn't have to turn away so many families at the beginning of every mission.

"You won't believe it, Pat," I explained, trying to appeal to her better nature.

"Kids are getting all these incredible operations—they're transformed. It's truly life-changing."

Patricia was not impressed. She was sitting in her comfortable office in Manhattan. All she cared about right now was meeting her deadline. But I wasn't about to hop on a plane and race back to Madison Avenue just because she was in a swivet. I didn't care if we lost the account. I think I may have even told her this in so many words.

We hung up on one another. Patricia was ticked off because she wasn't getting her ads; I was mad because she didn't have any idea how little those ads mattered in the wider scheme of things. In Thai Nguyen, we had three surgical beds going every day, each operating on about a dozen children. The pre-op and post-op wards were full. Everyone on the team was busy, exhausted, exhilarated. There were hugs, tears, smiles. Whether someone was helping or being helped, the experience was equally intense. The parents were so grateful, it made your heart ache. The goodwill and emotion that surrounded the mission was mind-blowing. This was life, drama, vital stuff. It made me feel alive. And it also made me suspect that everyone back in New York—my client Patricia included—was fast asleep or at best, sleepwalking.

I stood there in my phone booth after I hung up, trying to catch my breath. I rested my head against the wall in front of me. And that's when it hit me. This work here in Thai Nguyen mattered. It was my first inkling that I was spending my days doing something that, fundamentally, wasn't really helping anyone besides my clients and myself. As much as I'd feared the arrival of this epiphany, when it finally struck, I felt a strange kind of gratitude.

At the end of the five days, our quota of operations was complete. We were sad to leave, but energized by everything we'd achieved. There was a big farewell ceremony for us at the hospital. The mayor and the head of the hospital, all the local officials, the doctors and nurses, all the volunteers, posed for more photos for the paper.

The equipment was already being packed back into boxes and loaded onto a truck. We hugged and thanked all the volunteers, told them what a great job they had done. That day, I kept looking around for my friend Soccer Boy, but I couldn't find him anywhere. I asked around, but no one knew if he had gone home yet, or even if he lived in town.

A special bus was waiting to take us back to Hanoi. We climbed on board.

Everyone waved. As we pulled away, dozens of children began running to follow our bus, all of them waving goodbye, all of them shouting "Hello!!!!" I was waving from the back of the bus when I finally saw him.

"Look, there's Soccer Boy!" I said to the others on the bus. He was running with the others, trying to catch us, smiling and waving.

I smiled and waved even harder. Then I realized.

Soccer Boy still had his cleft.

What the...? What had happened? Why didn't he get the surgery?

DeLois Greenwood, who had organized the mission, was sitting right next to me. She'd seen him too. That little boy, running behind us, waving, as we left him in the dust. "What happened?" I asked her.

She didn't know. DeLois had been on dozens of missions before me. She had seen thousands of children turned away like this. There was nothing she could say.

I looked around again. I could still see him in the distance. He was still smiling. He should have been throwing rocks at us, but instead, he was smiling. This great kid, just accepting his fate, grateful that he got to kick a ball around with a bunch of phony Americans.

Nobody on the bus said a word.

I knew all along that we had to turn away children. I had heard the stories of how the other volunteers had to turn away mothers and their babies, breaking their hearts in the process. It made me sad, but it had never made me feel angry before. Until now, I was happy to toe the party line: Don't think about the ones you turn away. Think about the ones you help. This is the way it is. There's nothing we can do.

But Soccer Boy was my friend. This was different.

I kept thinking about Soccer Boy the whole way back to Hanoi. I no longer felt like the noble humanitarian with his name on all the microphones, smiling with his thumbs up for the cameras. Yes, we'd come to help children, but it was obviously a drop in the ocean. We had turned away so many families back there! Couldn't we do better than this? My business school brain was already working overtime. We had turned away more than half our customers. No company in the world would ever operate like this!

When I told others on the mission how I felt, I got the party line: Brian, we can't help everyone in a single visit. That's why we have to go back to the States and raise more money, so we can go on more missions.

The message was clear: I was the mission rookie. I was too sensitive, too naive. One day I would get used to this. The problem was, I didn't want to get used to it. That night I went back to my hotel under a giant cloud. I didn't like how any of this felt. I didn't like swooping in from on high, taking all the credit, and then not living up to the promise.

This wasn't what I had signed up for. Not at all.

.... FOUR ....

Teach a Man to Fish

The image of Soccer Boy kept chasing me long after our bus pulled out of Thai Nguyen. For me, it represented the dark side of what we were doing on the missions: for every hundred children that we helped, we were leaving behind hundreds of others. After my return from Vietnam, I was down and demoralized. Now that I had seen the limitations of these missions, I couldn't see the bright future I'd seen before. At the same time, I wanted to do more; to figure this out. What I'd learned while standing in that rickety phone booth in Thai Nguyen—while hanging up on one of my biggest corporate clients—was that this cause was becoming more important to me than anything else in my life.

In June of the following year, Mike and I sold our ad agency for more money than we'd ever dreamed we'd make in our lives. We still had to run it for the next two years, but that was easy compared to building up the company from scratch. We no longer had to chase new clients, and we didn't have to worry about the future. It was a stroke of incredible good fortune. I knew that I was financially secure, and that I could take my time figuring out what came next. I also knew I wanted to spend as much time as was necessary to solve the problem of how to help children like Soccer Boy. I didn't want to go on another mission until I'd had time to work this through. More and more missions meant more and more Soccer Boys. It meant families traveling hundreds of kilometers, only to be told, "there's no more room." What kind of company turns away half of its customers? Surely there had to be some way to help everyone.

I started to do the math, but it was daunting. How many children are born with birth defects all around the world every year? How many suffer with other types of deformities? How many of those children come from families who can't afford surgery? It had to be a number in the many millions. Our cost per surgery was in the thousands of dollars. Even at a very conservative estimate of three million children, we were looking at many billions of dollars to help everyone. That was more money that I would be able to raise in ten lifetimes. As I did the math, it became increasingly clear to me that the surgical mission model—while extremely noble—was not an ideal business model. The cost per surgery was way too high and we had to find a way to reduce it dramatically.

Operation Smile wasn't the only medical mission organization out there. In fact, there are hundreds of similar organizations doing reconstructive surgical work all over the developing world. Every month of every year, people from the Western nations going on medical missions to help needy children in some of the most remote places on earth. For these organizations, the solution has been "raise more money, so we can go on more missions." The volunteers and mission organizers I had met going to China and Vietnam had such good hearts, but I had a business economics brain. I didn't have a clue what went on in an operating room or how to run a medical nonprofit, but I did know how to create an organizational structure and match capacity with demand. With my background in high tech, I was also an innovation addict. I loved new ideas and new approaches to old problems.

So I kept thinking. Yet another seed had been planted in Vietnam. As I'd been roaming around the hospital in Thai Nguyen—asking my usual questions and taking my photos—I met the hospital's resident surgeon who was hanging out on the sidelines. Later, when I asked how much a surgeon in a rural hospital like this one got paid, I was told, "about $200 a month."

Now that I was back in the States, the thought went through my head, "Well, why don't we pay local doctors $400 a month just to do our surgeries, and we'll be helping a lot more kids and saving a whole lot of money?" It was so simple that I couldn't believe that someone hadn't thought of this before. Why were we spending $100,000 to fly everyone and all our equipment to Vietnam, when we could help Vietnamese doctors to perform the same surgeries for a fraction of the cost? The economics were really compelling. I calculated that the money spent on single mission could pay for a year's salary for forty Vietnamese plastic surgeons. It made sense in another respect too: in a world where the U.S. State Department issues travel warnings on a weekly basis, this would enable children to be helped anywhere, anytime, 365 days a year.

I decided to work from the ground up. I sat down with a blank piece of paper and began to sketch it out.

To me, the surgeries were a given. They were a proven cure: cheap, quick, 99.99% successful.

We knew the solution to the medical problems these children were facing. Our cure was reconstructive surgeries, already well developed and highly effective. Not every charity has their cure; we were lucky.

We knew where the vast majority of kids with untreated problems were in the world: developing countries.

And we knew how to raise lots of money. Our initial success was so encouraging. I was confident that with smart restructuring, we could raise many more millions.

The last piece of the puzzle—what we needed to make this all come together—was a new way to deliver the surgeries.

The challenge was to come up with a new cost-efficient business model that dramatically brought down the cost per surgery, which in turn would enable us to help every child who needed us, not just a chosen few. And if the surgery cost one fifth as much, we could help five times more children.

The next challenge was timing. Going someplace once a year for two weeks was an expensive band-aid that was never going to be economically feasible in the long run. The volume was too limited. We weren't going to solve problems that affect millions of children doing a handful of surgeries at a time. The model of parachuting Western doctors into these countries and then parachuting them out again was too constrained. We were never going to find a way to scale up using this model.

My mind kept going back to the surgeons in Vietnam making $200 a month. Local surgeons. Self-sufficiency. Give a man a fish, and he'll eat for a day. Teach a man to fish, and he'll eat for a lifetime. What if we could find a way for surgeries like these to happen every day, not just once a year? What if we could teach a man to fish?

Then I thought about how people deliver goods and services in developing countries. On bicycles, in buses, on trains.

And then it came to me.

We needed to put the mission on a train.

Developing countries run on trains. Millions of people and goods are transported around the developing world every single day. Right away, I could picture exactly how it would work. Our mission team flies into the country to meet the train. The team boards the train. The train sets out for its destination—the town we've chosen for our mission. Everyone in the town knows the train is coming. The circus has come to town! Everyone wants to come and see the train. Lots of excitement, great publicity, everyone knows that we're here. Kids with defects come from all over.

This train has a nice sleeping car where the mission volunteers can stay. It has an operating room car with a state-of-the-art OR where the surgeons can do their surgeries, safely, efficiently, and without having to fly out equipment. Then there's the classroom car. The classroom car is loaded with educational materials, medical equipment, manuals and software. Every town we visit, we bring local surgeons onto the train and show them how to do these surgeries. We train local surgeons on the train!

And there's one last car. This is the car filled with equipment and supplies and computers and special software and information. So when the train leaves town, we unhook the last car. Instead of packing up and taking every last Q-Tip home with us, we give these doctors everything they need to keep performing surgeries long after we've huffed and puffed out of town.

We create a self-sufficient model.

That was the big idea. Self-sufficiency. Put the mission on a train. Then put the mission out of business.

Once the train leaves—it doesn't need to come back.

I needed to get some input before I took this any further. I turned to DeLois, who by now was head of our New York chapter, and responsible not only for fundraising, but for organizing every mission we went on. She had been to 65 countries on missions. She knew more about this work than anyone, and I deferred to her better judgment completely. On the missions, it was usually DeLois who had the job of consoling the families when their children didn't make the list for surgery. She was a mother herself. It broke her heart to have to turn away families. And she had been doing this for years and years. If there was anyone who should have been frustrated, it was DeLois.

"This train idea isn't about helping twice as many kids, or ten times as many kids, or 100 times as many kids," I told her. "It's about helping all the kids. Every kid. It is about solving the problem forever."

DeLois looked at me quizzically.

"So what do you think?" I asked, expecting the worst.

And then DeLois smiled.

"I like it," she said.

"Really? You do?" I was expecting a litany of reasons why this wouldn't work.

"Yes," she went on. "I like the Johnny Appleseed part of leaving behind the equipment and training the doctors. It's the hardest part of my job, telling those mothers that there's no more room on the schedule. Every time we leave, we pack up everything and it always breaks my heart."

We decided to call the train, the "Smile Train."

The next step was getting potential funding for the idea, and I knew exactly whom I was going to approach. Charles Wang was one of my biggest clients at the ad agency, and one of the most successful high tech executives in America. The company he founded, Computer Associates, remains one of the largest software companies in the world. Charles is the ultimate self-made man, with a reputation as extremely driven and demanding, but for as long as I'd known him, I was aware that, despite his tough exterior, he had a serious philanthropic side. After I'd come back from the mission to China, I'd invited Charles to become an Operation Smile donor and board member, and he'd said yes. Now, my big idea was to test drive the train idea in China, Charles' homeland. The train was going to have technology at its core. I had a feeling Charles would love the train.

I started researching trains. I found out how much it costs to buy a train, run a train, how many people it takes to staff a train, how many can sleep on a train, how many it takes to keep it going, how many dining cars you need. I went train-crazy. Nothing I found out discouraged me. The more I learned, the more excited I became. The economics were incredibly compelling. I had a million spreadsheets that showed how many surgeries local surgeons could perform at what costs. I discovered we could probably do ten times as many surgeries for a tenth of the cost. I ran the numbers over and over again to check they were correct. I just couldn't believe what I was coming up with. Could we really help 10,000 kids in a year?

Before long, I was ready to present the concept to Charles Wang. I decided to keep it simple. Even though I had dozens of graphs and spreadsheets and PowerPoints I could have shown him, instead, I took with me a single sheet of paper. It was a photo of a train with giant faces of children and the words "SMILE TRAIN" emblazoned on the side.

At my next meeting with Charles, after we'd finished going through the new ads that my agency was creating for his company, I told him I had one last thing to discuss.

"Charles, on every mission we do, we turn away at least one kid for every kid that we help."

Charles didn't skip a beat.

"Well, that's dumb," he said.

"It is. And believe me, when you're there and you see these families, the mothers crying and begging for help, it's just terrible. Apart from anything else, it's not a good business model. We have to find a better way of delivering these surgeries."

"And?"

"I have a new idea that could increase the number of surgeries exponentially."

"Exponentially, Brian?" I guess by now he was probably used to my occasional exaggerations in pitch meetings. Even so, I held my ground.

"Yes, exponentially. And it would radically change the way we do our missions. The idea is a train."

Then I put the piece of paper with the picture of the train on his desk in front of him.

Charles' face showed no emotion whatsoever. Did he hate this or love this?

"This is a train that would travel around China. Our mission teams would fly to the train. We would do all our usual surgeries, but more importantly, these would become training missions. We would train local Chinese surgeons on the train. And then when the mission leaves town, we would leave behind the tools, technology and supplies they need to keep operating long after we go."

I stopped right there. Charles didn't need to hear any more.

He looked at the photo. He looked at me.

"I love it," he said.

"You do?"

"Yes. There's just one thing. Why do you need to send American doctors to China to do the training China has plenty of good surgeons. Have you ever seen what we can do with chopsticks?"

We both laughed. The joke broke the tension. And Charles had a good point. Of course there were probably incredible surgeons in China. Okay, this was going well! I began packing up my things to leave, before Charles found some reason to change his mind.

"I'm going to come back to you in a couple of weeks with a more detailed project plan," I told him. "This is big. This could change the lives of tens of thousands of children."

"Tens of thousands of children, Brian?"

"Yes!" I protested, assuming he was accusing me of exaggeration again. In fact, he was setting me up.

"Well in that case," said Charles, "I will give you ten million to get this good idea on the tracks."

I was dumbfounded.

"10 million…dollars?"

"Yes, $10 million dollars," repeated Charles, matter-of-factly, as if he telling me that he wanted to give me a ham sandwich.

I tried to remain calm. Now it was my turn to double-check.

"Really, Charles?"

"Yes," he nodded.

"Wow." This was all I could say. I wanted to hug him, but he wasn't that kind of guy. It's a rare occasion when I find myself speechless, but this was certainly one of them.

"Thanks, Charles. I don't know what else to say."

"Don't say anything," he said. "Get to work."

That $10 million pledge took the idea from a concept to a feasible program. What's more, it was a huge confidence boost. I felt that if Charles, one of the smartest guys I knew, loved the idea, then this was an excellent start. I flew down to Virginia to meet the Operation Smile Board, to present the idea of the Smile Train. But the meeting did not go well. Some of the board members liked the idea, and understandably they were thrilled with the size of Charles's donation, but others, including Bill Magee, felt very differently. We were too focused on China; the concept was too big, too expensive. Apart from anything else, it might be dangerous.

Dr. Magee wanted to be certain that the kids he operated on were getting the highest standard of care, and he wasn't sure that local doctors in developing countries were up to it. And in many ways, I can understand why a surgeon would feel that way.

Patients' lives were in his hands. But I disagreed strongly about the quality of local doctors. I was convinced that, with a little extra training and financial help for medical supplies and equipment, children would get the same standard of care, if not better. Why would local doctors be any less capable than their Western counterparts, if given the support, training, and equipment they needed? If anything, I argued, local doctors have more of a stake in getting it right for their patients. They can't just pack up and jump on a plane when something goes wrong. They are there to build on the reputations of their clinics and hospitals.

"What about Dr. Han Kai?" I pointed out. This was a fantastic, skilled local Chinese doctor and a volunteer who had been on numerous missions with us. He was a talented surgeon, born and bred in China. I knew that Bill trusted and respected him.

In the end, the board decided to vote "yes," and Bill gave us the go-ahead to pilot the program. As it turned out, the idea had tremendous momentum. Not only had Charles Wang given us money, he also put his network of wealthy friends and influencers at our disposal. Everything started to move very quickly after that, and it was all very positive. Charles met with Bill Gates and over lunch, and Gates promised to give us $1 million. Charles met with former President George H.W. Bush in Texas to pitch him on the idea—Bush is revered in China, and Bush loves China. Bush promised to mention the idea when he saw Jiang Zemin, the President of China, who was coming to the U.S. for a major visit that fall.

Then, one day in early October 1997, Charles's phone rang: "Hello, President Jiang Zemin of China has heard all about your Smile Train idea from President Bush, and he would like to meet with you to discuss this venture."

This was a big deal. Zemin had scheduled only three private meetings during his visit to the U.S. This meant he really did like this idea. The problem was, Charles had plans for the 31st.

"Well, I would love to meet with the President but that day is Halloween and I promised my kids I would take them trick or treating—is it possible to meet with him on another day?"

Then there was a very long pause on the other end of the line. Charles was trying to reschedule the President of China! For a minute, he thought he had made a huge mistake. Then he heard:

"How does the next day look for you?"

Charles flew out to L.A. and spent an hour with Jiang Zemin. He showed him dozens of pictures of Chinese children with defects and deformities, the pictures of the proposed train, the spreadsheet with projected surgeries. Zemin loved it all. At the end of the meeting, the President of China pointed to one of his twelve senior people huddled around the table and commanded, "Make this happen!"

The President of China had said yes! Truly, nothing else could stand in our way. We began making plans to launch our train project in January of 1998. It was heady stuff. Suddenly, our small non-profit had grown more than ten times in size, and its mission had grown even more in ambition. Charles upped his donation to $27 million, and found a matching donation for us from his mentor in Switzerland, Walter Haefner. Tom Brokaw offered us a spot on the Today Show. On the day we launched the program our press conference was attended by 100 reporters; our launch party was hosted by Ann Curry and attended by the Ambassador of China, Diane Sawyer, Carly Simon, and dozens of other luminaries.

I had come back from Vietnam under a giant cloud, but now the clouds had cleared and everything was looking up. We had a brilliant new idea. We had funding for it. And we had momentum and support that was building every day.

Then we met His Excellency Han Zhubin, Minister for Railways for the People's Republic of China.

This was supposed to be a logistics and planning meeting for the train project. Instead, it turned out somewhat differently from expected. We met with His Excellency one freezing morning in January of 1998. Our delegation from Operation Smile made our way down the longest corridor I have ever seen and into an enormous meeting room, painted red and gold, in the bowels of the minister's Beijing offices. We were shown to our seats—incredibly uncomfortable, elaborately carved high-backed wooden chairs. The temperature in the room was sub-zero, colder than a meat locker.

I was sure I was supposed to feel intimidated, but instead, I couldn't wait. Finally, this was the moment when our train was going to become a reality. While we waited, I set up my PowerPoint presentation on my latest, state-of-the-art laptop, complete with a digitally animated train whizzing through the Chinese countryside, pictures of smiling children emblazoned on the side. Everyone we'd told about the Smile Train so far went crazy for the idea. I was confident that Minister Han was going to feel the exact same way.

Finally, after we had waited for what seemed like an hour, Minister Han entered, followed by his retinue of twenty officials, assistants, and translators. He sat down at the long table in front of us, his minions on either side. More staff arrived carrying pots of jasmine tea, which they poured into tiny teacups for us. The tea tasted as if it had been brewing for days, and I wondered if the minister saved this potent brew for his foreign visitors in the hope its off-putting flavor would give him some kind of tactical advantage. Probably so.

Nonetheless, we kept drinking, because the tea was hot and the room was freezing.

We exchanged the usual round of introductions and pleasantries via the translator. I remember how desperately I wanted to get the small talk over with so we could get down to business. Eventually, the chitchat subsided. I jumped up, got my clicker, lit up the screen. I was determined to fill that cold room with enthusiasm and passion.

"This is going to be the most popular train in all of China!" I exclaimed. "When it comes to town, people will travel from far and wide. People are going to love it! This train is going to bring hope and life-changing surgeries to children who need it most. When the train leaves, it's going to leave behind smiles and goodwill. This is about Chinese doctors helping Chinese children. We will be training, we will be teaching, we will be donating equipment and computers and medical supplies. The Ministry of Railways would get so much credit for being a partner in this noble venture!"

Minister Han and his retinue stared at me blankly. Was the interpreter communicating everything that I said? It was hard to tell. Even so, I kept talking. I ended my spiel with a big photo of a Chinese girl, smiling from ear to ear. Then I gave the minister and his men my own big, bright grin, and waited for my round of applause.

Silence.

The whole line-up of Chinese officialdom stared at me. Then Minister Han cleared his throat, noisily slurped his tea, and started shouting in Mandarin, pausing occasionally so that his interpreter could keep up.

What the translator relayed to me, almost apologetically, was this:

"His Excellency the Minister wishes to inform you that it is his duty to move more than one billion people a day along single-gage railways. In order to prevent trains from colliding and causing much chaos to the infrastructure, it is necessary for the trains to stop in each station for no longer than 3.5 minutes. And you people are asking to stop a train for two and a half weeks in places where there is only a single track. With all due respect, His Excellency would like to know, are you out of your minds?"

Wait a minute. The whole time I'd been researching my Smile Train, I'd never once thought to ask if Chinese trains run on single tracks. Where the hell were we going to park our train while it was in the station?

There had to be a solution. In all my years in advertising, I'd been in so many meetings with unhappy clients and I'd always managed to turn things around. That day at the Ministry of Railways, I went into full scramble mode.

"Okay," I said, stalling slightly. "Minister Han. That is an excellent point about the tracks. Of course we don't expect to shut down all the traffic in a village for two weeks. Ummm, perhaps we can build a little side track where our train can sit without getting in the way?"

Admittedly I had not had time to fully develop my idea. The translator looked at me, as if to say, "Do you really want to say that?"

After this was relayed to Minister Han, the high official spluttered a mouthful of tea. I'm still not sure if he was laughing, or enraged. Then he explained slowly, as if to a child, that however noble our cause, we were asking the impossible. Our dream of helping children was his worst nightmare, and he wanted no part of it.

"But…but…Your Excellency, these children need you!" I ventured Minister Han continued, and the more he spoke, the more his voice started to rise. His face turned bright pink, and the veins on his neck started to bulge. Still speaking in rapid-fire Mandarin, he banged his fist down hard. Then the railway czar dropped the diplomacy act altogether. He spoke in English for the first time.

"You people are a pain in my.. ASS!"

This was the point at which I learned that Minister Han did speak English after all. I smiled politely. My mind was racing. What do I say now?

I had put a year of my life into developing the Smile Train, and I wasn't going to go down without a fight. Rational argument wasn't working. It was time to tug at the heartstrings instead. What could I say that would give Minister Han a lump in his throat and bring a tear to his eye?

I gave it my best shot.

"Minister Han, if you will allow me. In my country, there's a story that children read when they're young. It's a story about overcoming obstacles, about finding solutions and about never giving up. It's a story about a train, a little train that's looking at a big mountain and it has to somehow find a way to get over that mountain."

Minister Han was nodding. He was listening. I kept talking.

"As this train started up the mountain, pulling a very heavy load, much too heavy for its tiny engine, it started to slow down, but then this engine, this little engine, it kept saying to itself, 'I think I can, I think I can, I think I can.' And it kept going. It kept chugging. It didn't quit."

I paused. Now all the officials were nodding. They were rooting for our little train. I had them! "This engine is called: the Little Engine that Could…"

"Aha, I know that story," said Minister Han, speaking in English again.

"You do?" I asked, overjoyed.

"That's Chattanooga Choo Choo!"

67

"Hahaha," the minions fell about laughing. I tried to laugh along with them, but inside, I was crying. I knew it was over. It was clear that my little train story wasn't going to sway Minister Han. All my pictures of smiling children in PowerPoint presentations weren't going to change his mind. The Minister's job was to move more people on his trains in a single day than probably live in the entire United States. Of course he wasn't going to let our little train stand in his way

I left with my fancy laptop under my arm and my tail between my legs. I was in shock. Everything had gone so well up to now. Everyone loved this idea, former President Bush, even the President of China himself. The only person who didn't love the idea was the person who mattered the most. The Minister of Railways! Reality had finally hit. We weren't going to be able to put the mission on a train. I tried to think it through. Was I going to have to give everyone their money back? Wasn't there some other way of going about this? In many ways, the train itself was the least important part of the idea. In fact, the train was just the vehicle carrying the idea. What really mattered was the concept. Teach a man to fish. Chinese doctors helping Chinese children. The important part was promoting self-sufficiency. It didn't matter whether we did this on a train or a bus or a rickshaw.

Okay, I thought to myself, from this point onwards, our train is going to have to be a figurative train.

After we came back from China, though, it felt as if all our good energy and momentum was leaving us. Bill had been a reluctant supporter of the Smile Train idea, and after the China setback, he continued to express that he thought the whole concept was too risky. I flew down to Norfolk again and again trying to accommodate each new concern. Pretty soon, I began to realize that no matter what I said or did, there were major philosophical differences at work. Western surgeons have a long history of traveling overseas to operate on patients who wouldn't otherwise have access to care. This is a noble endeavor, and it's often extremely beneficial to patients, but only to a point. A mission is always finite. When the mission leaves, it's the end of the story.

We were suggesting a whole new approach based on self-sufficiency, building local infrastructure, and empowering local doctors to operate on patients 52 weeks a year, with the purpose of helping many more children. It's a critical question that every charity must answer at some point in its development: how do you scale up? How do you grow from being a small operation to an organization that can keep expanding and doing more? I felt that we needed to start running ourselves like the multimillion-dollar business we had become. This was a giant leap to make, and it demanded a philosophical shift on the part of its founders. I wanted us to embrace this new concept. But for whatever reason, I couldn't get Bill to agree. I didn't want to split with Bill; he had become a very close friend and a mentor. But we couldn't find the middle ground. Eventually we shook hands and decided to part ways. Operation Smile continues to do incredible mission work, helping children all over the world. Meanwhile, Charles and I took the money we'd raised and put Smile Train on its own tracks in August of 1999.

On the one hand, it was a relief to be going it alone. On the other hand, it was terrifying. We were starting from scratch. We had no staff, no offices, no program, and no experience of running a program like this one. What we did have was a blank sheet of paper..

.... FIVE ....

The Road Map

Charles and I decided to sit down together and create a roadmap, a way forward. We began by writing a list. We put on that list everything we liked and didn't like about non-profits and how they are run. As businessmen and as donors ourselves, we had plenty of opinions on this subject. We kept interrupting one another, there were so many things we wanted to put on that list.

"Charities spend way too much on overhead and bureaucracy!"

Like most people, we'd read all those newspaper articles about inefficient charities wasting donations. We definitely didn't want to end up another statistic in one of those articles. Instead, we wanted to focus on tight management and strategic spending. We wanted to run this non-profit like a high tech start-up born in a garage: with a small, very smart staff that worked like crazy.

"Charities are too unfocused, they try to be all things to all donors and as a result they end up doing many things not very well."

Many charities blow in the wind. If a donor gives them money to do a specific program, then they do that program. The problem is, it's really hard to do a good job when you're trying to be all things to all people.

"Charities never seem to have concrete goals or business plans. It's never clear what anyone's actually accomplishing."

You can't reach goals if you don't set them. And if you don't set goals, how can you evaluate results or measure results or outcomes?

I couldn't write fast enough. Charles kept saying, "Yes!" Write it down! We don't want to be like that. We don't want to make that mistake."

That's when we realized: we wanted to create a charity that didn't act like a charity. We wanted to manage our non-profit like a for-profit. We wanted a business plan. We wanted experienced employees and professional management. We wanted to set goals for ourselves and reach them. In short, we wanted to run a successful organization with clearly defined objectives. We wanted to make an impact, make a difference, and have the data to show for it. We wanted to be smart, lean, fast, creative, innovative, and effective.

That same day, we decided that we were going to allocate 100% of donations to the programs, with Charles agreeing to pay for all non-program expenses. With Charles footing the bill for our overheads, we had one of the world's most successful business executives holding us accountable if we became too bloated. We agreed we wanted a small professional staff of talented and highly effective people—not the low-paid under-qualified people and unpaid volunteers and student interns that you usually find at so many charities. We felt that high tech was our ace up our sleeve. By using technology, we could keep our head-count low while driving our productivity sky-high. We wanted to show the non-profit world that technology could make donations go much farther, and empower charities to do things they could never do before. Charles and I had worked together, using and developing technology to change some of the world's largest corporations. Now we wanted to use this same technology to deliver a real and proven social benefit.

Above all, we wanted to stay focused. We didn't want to blow in the wind and try to be all things to all people. We were a small start-up charity. There are many dozens of medical problems in the world that can be helped by reconstructive surgeries, and it was clear that we were going to be too small to tackle all of them. Instead, we decided to focus all our efforts and resources on a single problem and do it really, really well. We wanted to pick one thing and then to have a meaningful impact.

We chose clefts.

Clefts are the number one birth defect in most developing countries, a problem afflicting millions of children every year. And yet the cure is a given. There are so many problems in the world that don't have an immediate solution—that may require years of research and devotion to solve. But we already had our cure. We had seen with own eyes how this simple operation could transform lives and bring smiles to the faces of kids who had suffered for years. Children who had been ostracized, who were unable to go to school, and who might never be able to get a job, were given a second chance. After a cleft surgery, the whole family benefits, and by extension the community and society at large. We knew that the cost of this transformation was comparatively small, and that only a modest amount of equipment was required. And yet the ripple effect of the surgery was potentially enormous. All we needed to do, we believed, was to pioneer a cheaper more effective way to deliver the surgery, so that we could reach more and more children. We believed that Smile Train's "teach a man to fish" model was the new delivery system. By helping, training, and empowering local doctors to solve the cleft problem in their own communities, our plan was to create eventual self-sufficiency.

This was the big idea: fostering self-sufficiency, so that every baby born with this common defect would be able to have it fixed, right away, free of charge, all across the world.

We shook hands on it. It might take us ten years, maybe 15 years, but we felt certain we could do it. Solve it. Fix it. Forever. Just the way that smallpox has been eradicated, we wanted to eradicate unrepaired clefts. Our job was to work ourselves out of a job. Staying in business indefinitely would mean failure, because our continued existence would mean that we weren't helping enough kids.

This was our road map, our business plan. Now all we had to do was execute it.

With over four million children and adults with clefts, China—alongside

India—had the most clefts in the world. And so despite our disastrous meeting with Minister Han, China remained the logical place to start.

In the spring of 1999, I flew to back Beijing to meet the president of the China Charities Federation, the largest charitable organization in the country. It was the CCF that had recently been appointed by the Chinese government to funnel funds from overseas to charitable causes—what's more, they were already running a small national cleft program of their own, working with local doctors and hospitals. Clearly, they had connections and the credibility that we needed to get a foothold in China.

The president of the CCF at that time was a man called Yan Mingfu. He was 75 years old, a mountain of a man with a big booming voice, an enormous smile, and a heart to match. I brought out my PowerPoint again, minus the pictures of the train. Instead, I showed him our dream in its purest sense: empowering local doctors, to eliminating the cleft problem in China.

To my great relief, Mingfu didn't bang his fist. He didn't tell us no. He didn't tell us that this was impossible. Instead, his response was this: "Yes we can do this together. Your project is about Chinese doctors helping Chinese children. This is the kind of project we have been trying to do at CCF for years."

This trip to Beijing marked the true beginning of Smile Train.

Mingfu's personal story was remarkable. In the 1950s, he was Mao's personal interpreter for his meetings with Kruschev in Moscow. After the Cultural Revolution, however, he was sent to prison and placed in solitary confinement for seven years. Here was a man who knew five languages fluently, but who spent seven years in jail without saying a word. When he was finally released, it took some time before he could remember how to speak again. But despite his experiences, he wasn't bitter. He still loved China. So he went back to working for the government, and once again he rose through the ranks. Then the Tiananmen Square massacre happened. Mingfu sided with the students, and he was sent back to prison. Again, he was released, and again, he devoted himself to serving the Chinese people. He was appointed the Minister of Civil Affairs, and then took over running the CCF.

Throughout his life, Mingfu had been knocked down, but he kept getting up again. This man wasn't just a kindred spirit; he was an inspiration. Now at the end of his career, he was devoting himself to promoting charitable work all over China.

"Our mission is to teach China to have a loving heart again," he told me during our meeting. "Our mission is to help the Chinese people to care about one another again." We were lucky to find Mingfu. Here was someone who wanted to help children, but equally, who didn't want to waste any time. China's economy was beginning its period of astonishing growth. The entire country was coming up, and Mingfu was committed to helping its medical provision grow with it. "The mark of a civilized country is its ability to help its poorest and neediest," he pointed out. From our first meeting, we were in agreement: it wasn't enough to help a few hundred children. We wanted to eliminate the problem of unrepaired clefts in the same way that they had been eliminated in the U.S. That was the goal. Yan Mingfu pointed out that he was 75 years old, and that he might have to retire before that came to pass. Only half-jokingly, I made him promise that he wouldn't retire until we'd achieved our target. In fact, a few years later, he did retire, but not before he helped us to launch Smile Train.

We divided up the work: his job was to find the children with clefts. Our job was to provide the funding and support. After that first meeting, we went for dinner at a restaurant in Beijing. I stood up and toasted our new partnership.

"To the Smile Train and CCF partnership!" I declared. "Working side by side, shoulder to shoulder, we will help thousands of Chinese children receive not just a new smile, but a new life!"

I finished my toast just as a giant clap of thunder broke overhead. Everyone agreed that this was a very good sign.

Thanks to the CCF, we found our first ever Smile Train partner surgeon. He was a man named Professor Liu Jiang Tai, based at a hospital in a remote province called Qinghai, on the northeastern stretch of the Tibetan Plateau. Dr. Tai was an oral maxillofacial surgeon—someone who operates on the areas of the head, neck, face, jaws, palate and mouth—and the he community he served was made up mostly of subsistence farmers, depending on the mountainous land for food, building materials, everything they possess. In the spring of 1999, DeLois flew north from Beijing to Xining, the capital of Qinghai. What DeLois found was a world with barely any electricity or running water, without televisions or even a working radio, completely cut off from the modern world. Qinghai wasn't just remote; it was also desperately poor. It remains one of the most impoverished places in all of China, contributing a tiny 0.3% of the country's economy. By contrast to the tiny brick homes where the people were living, the Qinghai Medical College Hospital, where Dr. Tai worked was vast, but it had seen better days. Inside were large, long wards filled with old iron beds and sallow-colored walls. Despite this unprepossessing environment, DeLois had a strong sense that the staff here were committed, qualified, and excited to participate.

The day of her arrival, DeLois watched Dr. Tai perform a cleft operation on a child. The surgery went well. She stayed on to observe the post-op care. Everything looked good. "The problem here is not the surgery," Dr. Tai informed DeLois. "It is the backlog. We have a waiting list of hundreds of children waiting for free surgeries. We just don't have the money to provide them."

In Qinghai, as in the rest of China at this point in time, members of the peasant class had to pay for the entire cost of the surgery, more than most of them earned in an entire year. Here was a good hospital, with a qualified surgeon who had all the necessary training and equipment, but the patients were too poor to pay. Dr. Tai could only provide twenty free cleft surgeries per year through a grant he received from the CCF. The hundreds of other children born each year in this area with clefts put their names on the list, and waited and waited.

DeLois returned to New York, excited but nervous. We had put so much time and energy into our "teach a man to fish" concept that it was a leap of faith to begin partnering with an actual surgeon and a hospital. She was wavering.

"I think this could happen, Brian," DeLois said. "I think we can work with this hospital. I have a good feeling about this Dr. Tai and his team. They're in an extremely poor part of the world and their facilities are modest, but it's safe and they have experience. What do you think? Should we test them out?" I could tell she was nervous, but I was ready. I wanted to try out our idea to see if it was going to work. This was the only way to truly test the model. "How much longer are we going to drag our feet?" I asked. "There are children who need these surgeries and a doctor who can provide them. Let's give him the money!"

Meanwhile, our lawyers voted "no" to the partnership. "Who is this Dr. Tai?" they wanted to know. "How do we know they won't steal from us? How do we know that these children are going to be safe? Let's slow down. Let's learn more."

But I knew that with this attitude, we could wait forever. The lawyers had questions that were valid, but we were spinning our wheels while hundreds of children were waiting for surgeries that we had the money in the bank to fund. I wanted to sign up Dr. Tai and get him to started right away. He was already doing surgeries for the CCF. Why not get him to do more?

And so in spring 1999, we ignored the advice of the lawyers and Dr. Tai became our Smile Train partner. In return for the amount of his grant, he had to provide us with a patient chart for each surgery and "before" and "after" photographs of the patient, so we could see if surgeries had actually been performed and that the quality was good. We had a world-class medical advisory board in place to assess the charts for safety and quality when they came in. Even so, the question loomed over us: was any of this going to work? Were we making a huge mistake? Amongst our donors and supporters, expectations were so high that it was possible we were setting ourselves up for enormous failure. We'd fought so hard. What if no one wanted these surgeries? What if the surgeries weren't safe, after all? If we failed, then that would probably be the end of Smile Train. And on the other hand, if this worked—if we were successful in Qinghai, this remote and impoverished province on the other side of the world—then we would be able to say that the Smile Train model was feasible.

We held our breath. Within weeks, patient charts began arriving at our offices in New York. Every week, more charts arrived. It was as if a floodgate had opened. In our wildest dreams, we never expected such an immediate return. I remember one day looking at all those charts and thinking, "Every one of those charts represents a child whose life has been changed."

The CCF already had many more surgeons lined up for us that were participating in their cleft program. We pinpointed three more hospitals, in Gansu, Guangxi, and Hubei. We signed on these partners with the goal of 2,000 surgeries in total, expecting that it would take in the region of a year to fulfill this quota. By the end of six months, Dr. Tai and the other Chinese partner surgeons had already surpassed that number. We hired a manager in China to look after the program. Finally, our train was on the move. We learned that many other hospitals were waiting in line to become part of the program. So many Chinese surgeons had watched from the sidelines while American and European mission doctors took over their operating rooms before packing up and leaving a few days later. It was these local doctors who had provided the after-care for patients when the mission team left town. They were the ones left to pick up the pieces. Now they were being given a chance to provide additional surgeries for their patients on their own terms. "No mission doctors?" they asked CCF when they heard about this program from American. "Sign us up!"

We hired a manager in China to look after the program. Finally, our train was on the move. We were charging ahead. After so many of setbacks, missteps, and detours, Smile Train was finally beginning to live up to its promise, helping children, empowering doctors, making a difference. For over a year now, I had been giving my presentation about partnering with local doctors. So many times I'd stood up and told people, "With just a little help, local doctors will be able to do great things, and help so many children!" But until this point, my presentation had been an educated guess, just a dream. ll along we had been convinced that clefts were an economic problem that we could solve by working with local doctors. Now the Chinese doctors were proving that this was true. We didn't need to build clinics. We didn't need to fly in American doctors. We just had to help the doctors who were already there.

.... SIX ....

The Digital Advantage

"Teach a man to fish" was our founding principle and our rallying cry, but in the early days of Smile Train, the question remained: what kinds of educational opportunities were we going to provide for our doctors and how were we going to provide them? Neither Charles and nor I had any kind of background in medicine, and in many ways, this was a positive: it helped us find new solutions and fresh approaches to old problems. But when it came to educating doctors, clearly there could be no substitute for expertise.

Charles was from the tech industry. I was from the advertising world. We didn't know one end of a scalpel from another.

Luckily, we knew someone who did. The first phone call we made in those early days of Smile Train was to Dr. Joseph G. McCarthy, the Director of the Institute of Reconstructive Plastic Surgery at NYU Medical Center. I'd first met Joe during my time running the schools program in New York. Joe is a world-famous authority in his field, bar none. This is the man who edited the series of medical books that every doctor in the U.S. has to read in order to become a board certified plastic surgeon. If anyone knew about training surgeons, it was Joe. In 1999, we invited him to become the head of our medical advisory board, a group of extraordinary medical professionals who began guiding us in every aspect of our work, from helping us with establishing quality and safety protocols, to reviewing our standards and surgeries across the board.

Joe was in complete agreement that the role of Smile Train was to empower local doctors.

"We need this new approach," he told me. "Missions have their place, but they promote dependency. Self-sufficiency is the way forward. And the only way to achieve true self-sufficiency is through training local doctors."

Joe was also clear that when he spoke about training, he wasn't talking about educating surgeons from start to finish. "Medical training is a lengthy and involved process," he explained. "Before you move into a specialty like plastic surgery, you need a general medical education. In this country, it takes a minimum of eight years before you get to a point where you can even begin to train in plastics."

Clearly, there was no way we could provide a complete medical education to doctors from top to bottom. What we could provide—at least in these early stages of the organization—was ongoing education for doctors who were already qualified to do cleft surgery, either because they were plastic surgeons, or oral maxillofacial surgeons like Dr. Tai.

Joe explained to us that if we wanted to improve quality across the board, then we needed to start bringing our surgeons into contact with their peers at home and in other countries. We had to provide them with scholarships to attend international cleft conferences. We needed to hold symposiums, workshops, and one-on-one trainings. Our goal should be to create situations where surgeons could regularly congregate and share ideas. This is common practice for medical professionals in the West, but for doctors in the developing world—when money and resources are limited—cost and geographical location can become a barrier. We knew that many of our surgeons were going to be working in relative isolation, the only cleft surgeon at a particular hospital, and the only specialist in their field for many hundreds of miles.

"The most important element of ongoing medical education is bringing physicians into contact with one another," Joe explained. "When doctors have opportunities to learn in this way, the entire field moves forward, and everyone progresses."

Yes, we could host symposiums and trainings and grant scholarships, but what else could we do?

"There must be other ways to help surgeons improve and learn," I insisted.

Joe nodded. He went and pulled a huge textbook off the shelves, opened a page, and pointed at a diagram of a cleft filled with arrows, cuts, and stitches. The content meant very little to me; it was the medium that was interesting. The walls of Joe's offices were lined with books like this one: big, unwieldy, expensive medical textbooks. NYU had a huge and beautiful library filled with textbooks on every medical subject and sub-specialty imaginable. Immediately, I thought of the hospitals I'd seen in the developing world where, more often than not, the libraries were filled with empty bookshelves. When we asked the staff, "Where are all the books?" they told us that they had been lost or stolen, and that there was no money to replace them. Medical books are expensive, often costing many hundreds of dollars; so are subscriptions to the leading plastic and reconstructive surgery journals.

I knew nothing about training doctors, but I knew a lot about using digital technology to deliver services and information cheaply to a large number of people. So I came up with what I thought was a brilliant solution.

"What if we could take all the best content on the subject of clefts, whether it's text, video, pictures, or audio, and compile a CD that we would send around the world?" I asked. "Almost like the greatest hits of cleft surgery training!"

I was feeling quite pleased with myself, but Joe was shaking his head.

"If you really want to do state-of-the-art medical training," he said, "you should be thinking about creating virtual surgery software. You need to meet a plastic surgeon called Dr. Court Cutting."

"You actually have a surgeon called Dr. Cutting?" I asked.

"Follow me," said Joe.

Joe took me down into the bowels of NYU, where he introduced me to Court, one of the foremost surgeons in the field of clefts, who also happens to be a math genius and a computer-programming expert."

That day, I witnessed the astonishing 3-D computer models that Court was already using to plan and execute surgeries for children born with major skeletal deformities of the face and head. These models were enabling him to judge precisely how to realign the bones during his surgeries.

When we suggested the idea of creating some kind of educational training tool for Smile Train's surgeons in developing countries, Court was immediately intrigued. He was at a point in his career where major medical publishing houses were knocking at his door, asking him to write a definitive textbook on cleft surgery. But Court was hesitant. He was concerned that two-dimensional diagrams and depictions—the kind that Joe had showed me in his textbook—were far restrictive.

"Surgery takes place in three dimensions," Court explained. "A flat illustration will never do it justice. Meanwhile people are doing amazing things with 3-D animation. Why not apply it to surgical training as well?"

A few weeks later, when we received Court's proposal to develop a virtual animation-training program for Smile Train, we didn't hesitate to fund the work. Immediately, we began looking around for precedents, assuming that someone else must have had the same idea. This was 1999. Toy Story, the first feature length 3-D animated film had come out over four years ago and since then, animators in Hollywood had recreated everything from 3-D bugs to dinosaurs to entire worlds. Surely someone out there was working on 3-D animations of surgical techniques. But we discovered that 3-D animation had never been applied to the surgical realm before.

That meant that Court would be starting from scratch. He explained to us that in order to create the models for the animations, he was going to have to film and scan the faces of children with unrepaired cleft lips and palates— he would then use these facial models as the basis for the animated demonstrations. Court wanted to use older children, rather than infants, firstly because our doctors were most commonly treating older patients, but in practical terms, he was going to be using MRI technology to create the images, and the larger the child, the higher the relative resolution of the scan. It was clear that locating older children with clefts was going to be an impossible challenge if we stayed here in the U.S.—every child in this country has his or her cleft fixed in the first few months of life. With the help and guidance of our partner in China, the CCF, two children, a boy and a girl, were offered the opportunity to come to New York for their surgeries—an all expenses-paid trip, during which we would film them for the animations. For so many months I had been talking and studying the subject of clefts, holed up in my New York offices. It had been a long time since I'd met any of our patients. This was my opportunity to spend an extended amount of time with children suffering with this defect—it was a tremendous insight into the lives of these kids and their ability to endure against improbable odds.

Yi Yun and Xan Fu Wong had applied for free operations through the CCF because neither of them came from families with enough money to pay for surgeries. They had been placed on a waiting list, and told to do just that—wait. In the fall of 1999, when their families learned there was an opportunity for two cleft patients to travel to the U.S. to have their clefts repaired by one of the finest cleft surgeons in the world, they immediately gave their consent. DeLois flew to Beijing to bring the children to New York along with two Chinese chaperones.

Yi Yun was eleven years old, as quiet as a mouse, silently taking in her surroundings with wide brown eyes. Reflexively, she kept bringing her hand to her mouth to cover her defect, a single split in her upper lip that extended deep into the roof of her mouth. It was hard to look at Yi Yun, not because her cleft was such a blight on her beautiful face, but because of the wrinkle in her brow that said so much about how she felt. Xan Fu Wong was three years younger and Yi Yun's exact opposite in terms of temperament, boisterous and energetic, wriggling in his seat on the rare occasion when he was actually sitting down, and sprinting around when he wasn't. Xan Fu had a bilateral cleft, a double split in his upper lip. The first time I met him, I thought of Soccer Boy: like my friend in Vietnam, Xan Fu didn't let his deformity interfere with his ability to smile.

Both Yi Yun and Xan Fu were survivors. They had been abandoned as babies and had spent the first few years of their lives in Chinese orphanages, their parents too scared, too ashamed, or too poor to keep them. Perhaps their families hoped that in an orphanage the children would be cared for, and that their clefts could be repaired; we'll never know. What we do know is that every year, untold numbers of children like Yi Yun and Xan Fu end up in orphanages all over the developing world. Not every child survives this experience. It can take up to three hours to give a baby with a cleft a single bottle—in most cases, the defect impairs a child's ability to suck and swallow. Often, cleft babies burns as many calories as they consume because feeding is such hard work. Imagine how challenging it is for busy orphanage staff to devote enough time to feeding babies with clefts. If these infants don't waste away from lack of nutrition, then they often become so weakened that they're dangerously susceptible to disease.

Somehow, Yi Yun and Xan Fu had made it. Yi Yun was in an orphanage for three years before her uncle adopted her and took her into his home. Xan Fu was living with foster parents when we met him—it was difficult for him to be placed for adoption because most agencies won't register children with clefts that are unrepaired. Even outside of their orphanages, life was far from easy for Yi Yun and Xan Fu. When Yi Yun's adopted brothers and sisters left for school each day, she would stay at home, doing chores for the family. Her cleft made it difficult for her to speak or eat. The hole in her palate meant she suffered with ear infections, which at times affected her hearing. When she did say something—which was rarely—she did so in a muffled whisper. Eight-year-old Xan Fu had never been to school and as a result of his difficulties feeding as a baby, he was tiny. If you didn't know his age, you would have guessed he was five or six.

Neither child had never left their villages before, never been on an airplane before, never been to a major city before, let alone another country. They each reacted very differently to being away: Xan Fu became ever more extrovert, a ball of energy and excitement; Yi Yun retreated further into her shell, silently assessing each new situation, never straying far from her chaperone. In New York, the children instinctively stayed close, holding hands wherever they went. Yi Yun took on the role of the big sister, reprimanding Xan Fu when he wanted to run up and down the hotel corridors. Xan Fu looked for Yi Yun whenever she was out of his sight.

When their MRI scans were complete, the children were prepped for their surgeries. Court operated on both children personally. Xan Fu went first; then Yi Yun. As soon as Yi Yun woke up from her operation her first words were, "How's Xan Fu?" In fact, both surgeries had gone extraordinarily well. Immediately after the children came around—with their lips were still swollen and done up with stitches—they stared at their own reflections with expressions of confusion mixed with wonder. Now, instead of bringing her hand to her face to hide her defect, Yi Yun put her fingers to her lip to check that the repair was real. When he was given a mirror, even the irrepressible Xan Fu had reason to pause. He kept staring and staring, until he looked up at us and flashed the first unmitigated smile of his life. The courage and grace that both these children displayed during their time at NYU was extremely inspiring for all of us who were lucky to meet them.

After their follow up scans were complete and they had fully recovered, the children boarded the plane back to Beijing to return to their homes. Their scars were healing. Their faces were transformed. They were going to enroll in school for the first time. The could begin their lives again. Xan Fu moved multiple times in the years after his surgery and the CCF lost contact with him, but the organization stayed in touch with Yi Yun. Today, she works in an electronics factory in Ghangzou. She is twenty-three. The little girl with the cleft lip has grown into a beautiful and confident young woman. Her scar is so faint as to be imperceptible; the wrinkle in her brow is gone. She no longer struggles to speak. She loves to cook and hopes to open her own restaurant some day. Her cleft is a distant memory.

Back in China, Yi Yun and Xan Fu could put their clefts behind them, but the images of their unrepaired clefts have gone on to have a lasting legacy. Thanks to the children, Court could begin creating 3-D models to animate a huge range of surgical techniques and ideas. He hired a talented animator called Aaron Oliker who was just out of college to work with him on the project. Together, they started writing new code for the 3-D animation program, Maya, adding functions to the software that would allow them to recreate the techniques in incredible detail. Animators have always played around with the human form—stretching out an arm like a piece of elastic, making a concertina out of a punched nose—but until now, they had never cut into the skin of the face, nor had they moved sections of the face around from one position to another, as happens during cleft surgery. It was slow and painstaking work and Court warned us to be patient. The DVD was going to be some years in the making.

In the meantime, we began developing another project designed to put information into the hands of our surgeons. We figured that in a digital age, there was no reason why a doctor should be working with a library filled with empty shelves. We didn't need to ship enormous, expensive medical text books all over the world. Instead, we approached every leading medical journal, asking them to find articles related to clefts going back fifty years. We persuaded them to donate this content to us, then we digitized it and organized it so it was searchable, before making it available free of charge on the web. The idea was that doctors and families of cleft patients should be able to visit our online library, obtaining information that would never otherwise ever be easily or freely accessible, no matter where they were in the world.

When Charles and I had drawn up our roadmap, we'd agreed: technology was going to the defining factor in growing the Smile Train model, enabling us to deliver services to more people, to drive up productivity, and to keep costs low.

In these early days, we were locating that place where medical expertise and digital technology intersected. In doing so, we were also finding the ace up our sleeve.

.... SEVEN ....

The Reluctant President

We were convinced that the model that was working in China could be replicated elsewhere. Now it was time to scale up: to start reaching not just 2,000 patients, but 200,000 patients. When Charles and I sat down and mapped out the blueprint for Smile Train, we were confident that we knew exactly what we were doing: that we could reach these children wherever they might be, and stamp out unrepaired clefts forever. And then two years later, we realized that we had already failed at our most important job as co-founders: we couldn't find the right president to run the charity.

We had the money. We had the big idea. We were off to a good start. We just didn't have the right guy at the helm. Our first president was a nice man, with plenty of non-profit experience. He was intelligent, talented, and committed, but we didn't feel he was moving the program forward in a way that was going to take us to the next level. We parted ways.

Charles and I began an exhausting, five-month-long search for the right guy.

Our second president was another guy with extensive non-profit experience, but he only stayed for fourteen months. We had chosen to pay our staff market-rate salaries for a good reason—we wanted to get market-rate results. As a result, we were determined to hold our employees accountable.

For the second time in two years, we were without a president. It was a low point. I told Charles that I was beginning to wonder if we were crazy. Maybe it was impossible to run a charity like a business. Maybe charities had their own culture and set of unwritten rules that businesspeople like us would never be able understand.

"This is getting ridiculous," Charles told me. "We can't keep hiring new people. Here we are nearly three years into this, and we don't have our act together."

"I know," I said. "I'm frustrated. We're wasting money, and worst of all, we're losing time when we could be helping kids." "I have an idea," Charles said.

I braced myself.

Charles was smiling, so this made me even more nervous.

"Why don't you run this damn train yourself?" he asked.

"Me?" I was shaking my head before the word was even out of my mouth. "No way. I really don't think I'm cut out to do this…"

"Why not?" Charles said. "You know what we want to do better than anyone. You've been here since day one. Plus, you move fast. You and I have worked together for twelve years now. Nobody you hire is ever going to live up to our expectations…"

Instinctively I shook my head "no."

"You've been saying for months now that you're looking for the next hill to climb," Charles pointed out. "This is your hill."

It was true that I'd sold my ad agency and was trying to figure out what to do next with my life, but running Smile Train? I was an entrepreneur. I was going to start up another company and sell it again a few years down the line. Charity work was my sideline, not my profession.

If I was honest with myself, I also knew I was too scared to go there. What if I took the job and discovered that it wasn't so easy after all, that it was hard or even impossible—what was I going to do then? What if I had to fire myself?

It was a sobering thought. The idea of taking the job and failing was daunting.

I told Charles I would think about it, buying myself enough time to come up with a good excuse for saying "no" and a good plan for finding our third president.

When I got home I told my wife about Charles's bright idea. "Home" at this point was a suburb in Long Island—my days in the Manhattan fast lane were finally over. I'd recently turned 40, sold the Porsche, gotten married. Recently, my wife and I had had our first child.

"Can you believe it?" I asked my wife. "Charles Wang thinks that I should take over as Smile Train's president!"

My wife's name is Kristen, but even since she was a baby her nickname has been Cricket. The epithet is appropriate. From the moment I met her, Cricket became my conscience, the bug on my shoulder reminding me of my better self. "I agree with Charles," Cricket said without skipping a beat. "You should take the job. You'd be good at it. It's in your blood."

"Yes, but…" I stammered.

"You keep talking about starting another agency and selling it again," Cricket said. "But Brian, at some point, you're going to have to ask yourself: do you really care enough to make it happen?"

I had met Cricket right around the time that we had launched Smile Train. Since then, she had watched me become more and more involved with the organization. She had seen how the work had changed me: how marriage and fatherhood had changed me. All of these factors had fundamentally reset my values. Cricket knew this about me. She knew that Smile Train was my private obsession. She knew how much time and energy I was already devoting to this cause.

As we spoke, Cricket was holding our daughter Maura on our lap. Maura was seven months old, just starting to smile herself. Maura, named after my sister.

"You don't have to do the job forever," Cricket pointed out. "Do it for a year, see if you like it. Besides, just think how proud our little Maura would be to have a Dad that does something besides make money." Cricket's words destroyed what little resolve I had left. I knew she was right. I was in the rare position of being offered a chance to do something that was bigger than making money, and I had the personal financial means to be able to say "yes." What kind of fool says no to that kind of offer?

I called Charles the next day and told him I would step in as interim president for one year, just to set the thing up and get us on track.

Charles was happy. I figured that in a year, I could create our business model, then hand off to the next president and get on with my career as an entrepreneur.

Walking into the office my first day on the job, I knew I had a challenge on my hands. Everyone had loved the outgoing president. I think the staff expected that heads were going to roll. Meanwhile, the place was a mess. Boxes were everywhere; papers were everywhere. The office looked like a college dorm rec room. People were wandering around doing God knows what. The only person I really knew was DeLois, and even DeLois seemed nervous.

I called a meeting and asked everyone to describe what exactly what their respective jobs entailed. By the end of the meeting, it was obvious that we had a great team of well-intentioned, talented, committed people, but no one had a clue what they were supposed to be doing or how they were supposed to be doing it. There was no organizational chart, no strategic plan, no procedures, no goals and objectives, no evaluations.

I called meeting after meeting. I kept asking questions.

"Who are our customers?"

"What are our product lines?"

"How do we market Smile Train?"

Most of the staff members at this time came from a non-profit background: they would sit and listen to me with a look of concern on their faces.

One of them, a young woman I'll call Kate, was very vocal when she heard something she didn't like.

"Brian," Kate said, "I have to say, it really offends me when you call the patients our customers. Why can't you just refer to them as patients?"

"I tell you why," I explained. "Because when we stop thinking about our patients as poor little kids on the other side of the world and start thinking of them as customers, we've taken the first step in giving them the respect and status they deserve."

We all could agree that our patients deserved the highest level of care, and they needed to get this care as soon as possible. By thinking of our patients as customers, I explained, this was going to help us think about how we were going to deliver services to them in the same way that a business would deliver products to a consumer. This wasn't just a clever analogy; it was going to help us become more strategic and goal-orientated.

"In the same way that we needed to think about our patients as customers, we need to think about our program in terms of product lines," I went on.

"But we're a charity," Kate blurted out. "Charities don't have product lines!"

"That may be the case, but what I'm saying is that charities absolutely should have product lines."

I began breaking down our product lines.

"Our first product is our partner hospital program where a hospital performs surgeries and we share the cost, so they can do many more surgeries than they were doing previously. They send us a patient chart, which in effect is like an invoice. We inspect it and then we pay it. Just like in a business."

People around the table were scratching their heads, looking confused.

"Our problem is that we have just one product, and yet we have many kinds of hospitals wanting to work with us. Some are big, some are small, some might be under-equipped, some might be fairly well equipped. We need to have more products so we can help all these hospitals, not just the ones that already meet our criteria." A hospital that didn't meet our high standards might want to apply for a small one-time treatment grant to help the staff buy equipment or hire an anesthesiologist. Maybe by offering treatment grants, we would be able to get to know that hospital before we turned it away.

"Well, that part of it I like," Katie conceded. "We've been turning away a lot of hospitals because they don't meet our standards."

"That's because we only have one product!" I couldn't resist.

"Yes, Brian," Kate conceded. "We only have one product." "Kate," I said. "What successful business only has one product?"

I moved onto my next thought.

"Meanwhile, we need to build the partner program just as we would any other franchise. We need to put protocols in place for every step of the process: how are we going to find hospitals, vet them, negotiate with them, partner with them, motivate them, compensate them, and monitor them. This is the way that Subway would do it. The way GM would work with their car dealerships. It's the way that you make sure you reach the largest numbers of people, while maintaining control of the quality of the service."

Various people tapped their pens, and an earnest young man in the corner rolled his eyes. I didn't blame the staff for feeling confused. They were from the caring professions; they had degrees in social work and psychology and nursing. This was all well and good, but in order to achieve our goal of eliminating unrepaired clefts the world over, we needed to think big and act fast. In other words, we needed to think and act like good business people.

"If everything goes to plan, we're going to be increasing our numbers of surgeries substantially in the coming years—this is going to raise its own issues for us in administrative terms." I told the staff about how I'd asked our partners in China to send me samples of patient records and photos for use in some marketing materials I was putting together. When I noticed the FedEx bill for $200 to ship these records, it set my mind racing. In everything I do, I always question cost—it's a fundamental business practice.

"How much is it costing us per month to ship patient charts in order to assess them for quality?" I asked the team. "How are we going to manage all these charts? Where are we going to store them? What are we going to do when we have 10,000 patient charts, 100,000 patient charts, 1 million patient charts? How are we quantify and assess all this data as more and more surgeries are completed?"

It didn't take a genius to see that we had to develop a digital patient chart and patient database. I knew the applications that could help us because I'd been creating database advertising for Charles Wang's Computer Associates since 1994.

"The price tag for going digital will be high," I warned the staff, "but it's going to save us thousands of dollars in the long run. And we need our capital investments to align with our strategic goals."

In the meantime, we needed to find more partner hospitals. A lot more partner hospitals.

"How do we find these hospitals?" I wanted to know.

"I'm guessing you're going to say advertising," Kate answered.

"Absolutely. Let's put together an advertising campaign that can run in the relevant medical journals. Let's write letters to every plastic surgery society in the world. Let's make contact with every Minister of Health in every developing nation in the world..."

Someone pointed out that there was going to be a big cleft lip and palate congress coming up in Sweden in a month.

"A cleft trade show!" I exclaimed. "Great. Here's where we can launch our product line worldwide. Here's what I want you to do. I want you to rent the largest booth and book the biggest restaurant in town. Smile Train is going to host a dinner for every surgeon coming to the congress. Then tell them we will sponsor the symposium if they let us give the keynote address."

The conference in Sweden was going to be our coming-out party on the international medical stage. More than one member of the staff remained unconvinced. This conference was going to cost us a lot of money—throwing dinners, hosting symposiums, buying airfares. It wasn't the way that the team was used to working: they were used to cutting corners to save money, being penny-wise but pound-foolish. It all sounded pretty extravagant to them. And yet I believed this was spending that was aligned with our goals.

And it worked.

We came back from Sweden with an address book filled with new contacts. We met cleft surgeons from all over the world. We saved ourselves months of flying around meeting with people individually, and a huge amount of money in the process. This was also a big step in getting the staff to trust me. Kate had been on the trip; she had seen first-hand the impression we'd made on the surgeons. She saw that these doctors wanted to work with us. They wanted to partner with an organization that had promised to empower them, train them, and give them a place on the world stage. In meetings, Kate no longer looked at me like I was the big bad wolf about to blow down the house. I think she realized that we had goals and targets, that I was absolutely going to hold the staff accountable for their work, and that results are important—not because you have a boss who's cracking the whip, but because every partner hospital that comes on board means more children that you're able to help. Yes, the staff was reluctant at first, but before very long, we were all energized and motivated by this approach. That first year running Smile Train, I learned that while this work requires compassion, it also demands innovation. We had to keep thinking of new ways of tackling old problems. We needed to adapt to each new challenge, rather than failing the smallest hurdles. I wanted us to stay smart, to innovate, to thrive on change. More than anything, I wanted us to stop dragging our heels and to start helping more and more children. The first year flew by. When we did the tally for our annual board members meeting, we discovered that although our number of surgeries the previous year had been 6,000, our partner surgeons had since fulfilled 30,000 surgeries. Meanwhile, we almost doubled our numbers of treatment partners (product number one). We introduced treatment, education, and training grants. We tripled our numbers of doctors trained. We added new countries to our list at the rate of two per month. We tripled our number of donors, taking annual fundraising from $311,000 to just under $1 million. I write this not to bang my own drum, but to show that by using simple business economic approach, by motivating staff, by holding them accountable, and by harnessing technology, a very small group of committed people had begun to have a real impact.

We were realizing that this was the right idea at the right time. All over the non-profit world, people were waking up to the idea that the existing models of aid weren't necessarily working. The medical mission model of flying in Western doctors on "surgical safaris" —although honorable—felt out-of-date and even patronizing to local surgeons who were more than capable of helping their own communities. The time-honored tactic of dropping in aid and resources to developing countries could only ever have a temporary impact. In the long term, the goal had to be self-sufficiency, building local infrastructure, education, and working in partnership with doctors on the ground. The gap between the health provision in the West and in the developing world was extremely wide, but our small, committed team was determined to prove that with skills, resources, technology, and innovation, it was possible to change that.

As it turned out, the position that I thought was beneath me, that I thought would be boring and dull, was more stimulating, challenging, and exciting than any job I'd ever had. I was hooked. I was using every skill I'd learned in my years in advertising, except that I was using those skills to help others. Making money seemed easy by comparison. Making a difference was harder, but it felt better. I'd spent a year convincing the staff that a charity was just like a business. In fact, what the staff taught me was that a charity is very different from a business in one important respect. In business, the mission was all about the money. With Smile Train, the mission was only about the children. I had found a new "bottom line"—numbers of surgeries delivered. Each surgery represented a smile that had gone out into the world, and a life changed. What other job could be better than that? After my year as interim president was over, I didn't leave. In fact, I hung on tight.

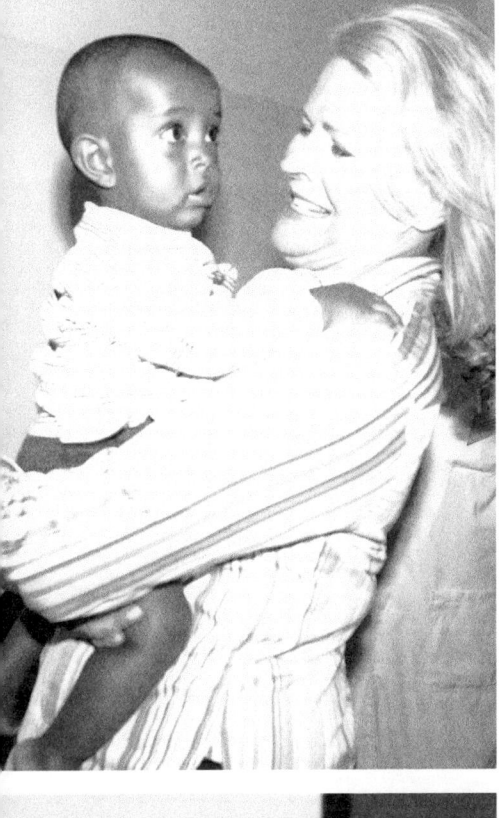

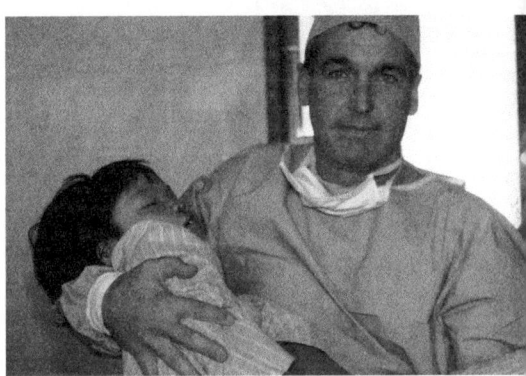

previous page
Brian pictured with his sister, Maura.

clockwise from top left
Candice Bergen, longtime supporter and member of ST Board of Governors, with cleft patient in Ethiopia.

TV star, Chris Meloni, traveled to Haiti with Smile Train and observed the surgery of 4-year old Bergeline.

Brian bringing 9-year old Colorful Cloud to post-op ward. Shezhen, China, November 1995.

General Colin Powell at Smile Train's 10th Year Anniversary said, "There is nothing quite like Smile Train."

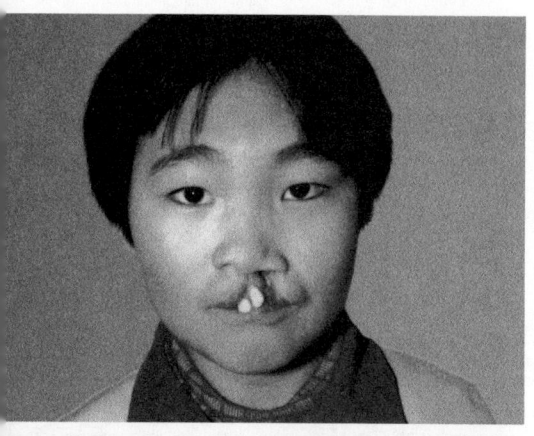

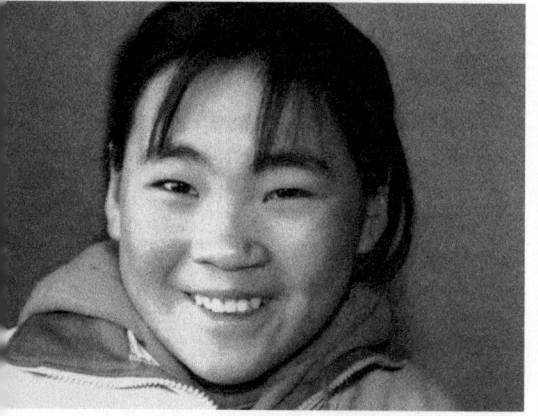
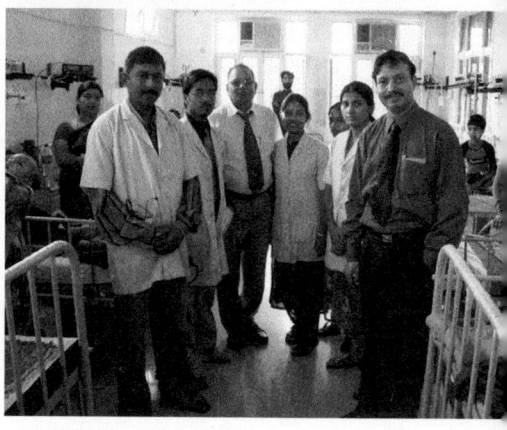
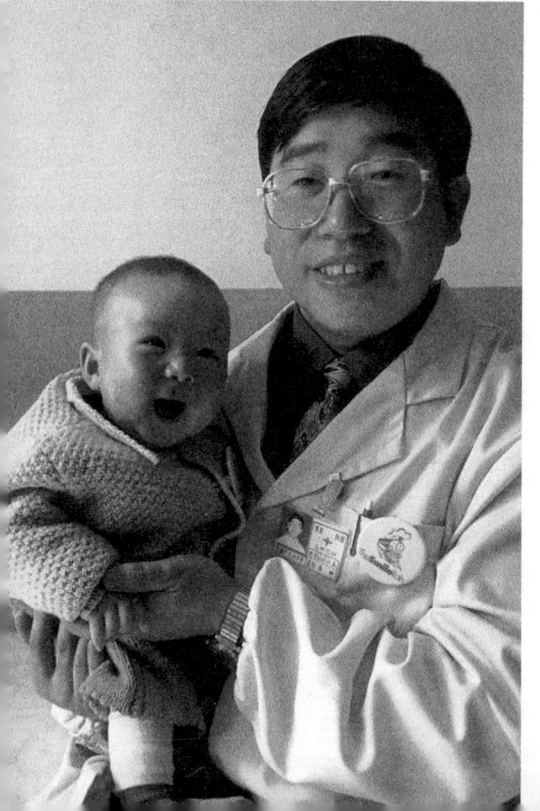

clockwise from top left
Smile Train Patient #1: 9-year-old
Wang Li from Likou, Jiangsu, China.

Dr. Hirji Adenwalla has performed thousands of free cleft surgeries for Smile Train in Southern India.

Smile Train partner, Dr. Subodh Singh and his team at GS Memorial Hospital, provide 3,500 free surgeries a year.

Smile Train's first partner surgeon, Dr. Liu Xinhua of Jinzhoung, Shanxi, China.

clockwise from top right

6-year-old Georgie Exarchakis, an American cleft patient, has raised $29,315 for Smile Train.

Smile Train Program Manager, Satish Kalra, built a 50,000 surgeries-a-year program while working out of the second bedroom of his apartment in New Delhi, India.

Brian on Operation Smile mission and "Soccer Boy." Bac Thai, Vietnam, November 1995.

Pinki and Brian the day after Smile Train's film, Smile Pinki, won the Oscar. February 2009.

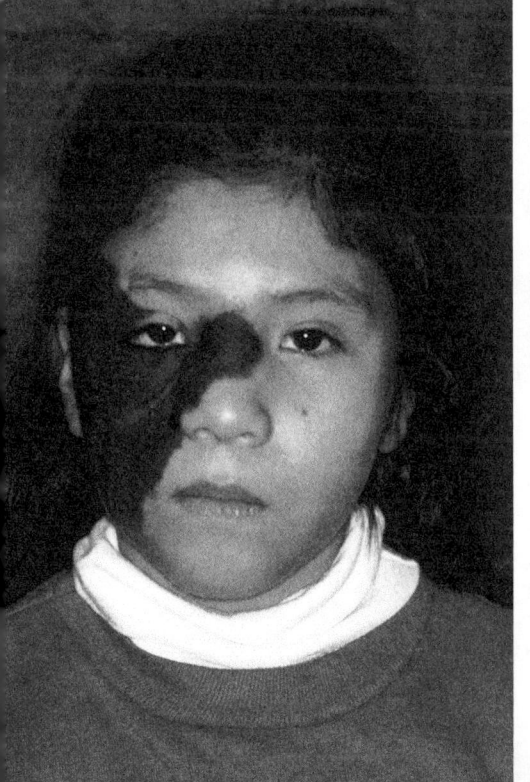

.... PART TWO ....

AFTER

.... EIGHT ....

A Tale of Two Doctors

The saying goes that a journey of a thousand miles begins with a single step. My journey as president of Smile Train—taking me to every corner of the developing world, and across hundreds of thousands of miles to some of the poorest and most remote places on the planet—began with a single trip.

My visit to India in November 2001 was my first time traveling as president of the organization. I was nervous. In fact, I would have much rather stayed home. A month and a half after the terrorist attacks on the World Trade Center in New York—an event that I'd witnessed from the window of our offices on Madison Avenue—and like everyone else in America, I was still in shock. No one wanted to travel. No one wanted to go anywhere. My wife had just given birth to our second child; she didn't want me to leave. How many foreign mission groups must have canceled their travel plans in the months after 9/11? Despite my deep reluctance, it was clear to me that I had to go to India as planned. Smile Train wasn't my hobby anymore; it was my job. We had seven partners in India waiting to meet us. What kind of message would it send if I didn't show up?

And so after twenty-hours in the air, DeLois and I landed in Chennai, on India's east coast. Stepping out of that airplane was like stepping into some kind of rapidly flowing torrent that carried us along for the rest of the trip. This was my first time in India and nothing could have prepared me for the intensity of the place, the sights, sounds and smells, the constant noise and dust, and the insane amount of traffic. The streets of Chennai were thick with buzzing motor rickshaws, rickety old bicycles, donkeys pulling carts, crazily painted trucks, entire families traveling on scooters and motorcycles—and always a stray cow stopping traffic. Wherever we went, barefooted children found us, tugging on our clothing, holding out their hands for a few rupees. My daughter Maura was a toddler by now; and here were children the same age, weaving through the rush hour traffic, their tiny knocking hands on the windows, rapping against your heart. We learned that over 18% of the population—that's 820,000 people— live in slums in Chennai and many thousands of others live out on the streets. At night, we saw fires by the side of the roads, from the homeless trying to cook food, glowing in the darkness.

We visited seven hospitals and met as many surgeons on our travels, all of them extraordinary in their own ways, but I'll describe two of them here. The first is from a new generation of young surgeons in India paving the way; and the second is from an older generation that helped to pioneer cleft surgery in this part of the world—each united in their commitment to help impoverished children with this defect.

Our first stop was Sri Ramachandra Medical College and Hospital in Chennai. The hospital was large, even by Western standards, made up of two tall towers of equal size joined in the middle. One tower was for people who could pay for treatment; the other was for those who could not. This had been our first criterion when selecting our partner hospitals—they should have a tradition of working with poor patients, a very good indicator of credibility.

The director of the plastic surgery department at the hospital, Dr. Jyotsna Murthy, was there to greet us. I'll admit, when I pictured our partner surgeons back, I usually had an image of an older doctor in mind, inevitably male. Dr. Murthy, meanwhile, was in her thirties, wearing a bright blue sari, her long dark hair tied back from her face and a look of clear determination and quiet intention in her eyes.

That morning, Dr. Murthy explained to us that her hospital was celebrating our arrival with a "Smile Train Day." The local press had been invited, along with cleft patients and their families for the celebration. She led us to the room where the gathering was taking place, and as we walked into the room, I caught my breath. Waiting for us were the families—mothers and fathers, babies, toddlers, older children, teenagers—every child holding a "before" photo showing how he or she used to look. The beautiful, smiling children were unrecognizable from their photographers. They came up to me. One by one, I shook their hands. I looked at their photos. I patted them on their backs. I shook their parents hands. I was knocked sideways by the experience. I couldn't believe how young some of the mothers were. They were still girls themselves, just 16 or 17 years old. One of them told us that she had always been blamed for her child's cleft because she had held a knife during an eclipse while she was pregnant.

"These doctors have saved her life," she repeated over and over.

Another young woman explained to us that she had been forced to flee her home—her mother-in-law threatened to throw the baby boy in the river because she believed he was cursed, that he was bearing the karma of his ancestors' sins. Her child been called "Hottaki"—the Hindi word for "cut lip"—since the day he was born until the day his cleft was repaired.

The superstitions and old wives surrounding clefts were fantastical, yet the suffering they caused was very real. Dr. Murthy told us stories of parents who had prayed their child had never been born at all. There was so much misinformation. This had happened to the child because the mother was unfaithful. She ate the wrong thing, did the wrong thing, laughed at the wrong person. Dr. Murthy had become an expert at dispelling such myths, carefully explaining to families that this was a very common birth defect.

"One in every 350 babies in India are born with this deformity," she reminded them. "You are not alone."

The reporters in attendance that day wanted to ask questions and take photographs. To my relief, they were much less interested in DeLois and I, and much more interested in Dr. Murthy, her team, and their patients. This was their program, their work, their hospital. I was extremely happy to be incidental.

Dr. Murthy explained to the local reporters that from her early days as a student, cleft surgery had been her passion.

"I remember my seeing my first cleft surgery when I was studying plastics in Mumbai," Dr. Murthy told the reporters. "The cleft was so horrible. When you look at a young child, you should smile at that child. But this cleft affected my entire reaction to looking at the baby's face. I felt terrible. I wondered what that does to a child, when everyone wants to turn away, when no one wants to smile at you. How does that make you feel? People say that no child dies of a cleft, but I believe a child with a cleft dies a hundred deaths every day."

Before partnering with Smile Train, Sri Ramachandra hospital had been doing the very best that it could to treat patients with clefts. Dr. Murthy could offer these children free beds. She could offer them free surgery. There was one problem: her patients were required to contribute the equivalent of $20 for disposable medical materials, such as bandages, gloves, and sutures. And for the vast majority of Dr. Murthy's patients, $20 was far more than they could afford. "I've had mothers fall at my feet, pleading with me to operate on a child," Dr. Murthy explained. "I would do all that I could, begging and borrowing materials to help them. But ultimately, there were patients I had to turn away. Our hospital was only been able to do so much—the need for our services here is so great. There were times when I would feel as helpless as the mother."

At the beginning of the partnership, Smile Train had agree to share the cost of 500 hundred surgeries to be completed over a period of twelve months at Sri Ramachandra.

"I told Smile Train I wasn't sure," Dr. Murthy remembered. "At this point, I was doing about thirty to fifty cleft surgeries a year. Where was I going to find 500 patients?" Reluctantly, Dr. Murthy agreed to the 500.

Sri Ramachandra began distributing pamphlets about the program. They pasted posters. They placed radio and newspaper advertisements. Word began to spread. Patients began to arrive. Dr. Murthy started to realize that it was possible that she had been wrong, that the need was greater than she'd ever imagined.

"Parents have brought their children to us from hundreds of kilometers away," Dr. Murthy. "They sell everything they have or borrow money to come here. The travel on buses, on trains, and on foot, because this is the only place where they know they will be considered for treatment."

In India, hospitals with specialist departments like Sr. Ramachandra are in the big urban areas. If you live outside of a major city, then you only have access to the most limited types of medical provision—usually a small health clinic run by local health workers. This means that patients who need surgery or anything more sophisticated than simple medication have to travel to the big towns to be treated. Earlier in the year, Dr. Murthy guessed that she needed to extend her reach. She'd been right.

She had begun working with government agencies in the smaller cities surrounding Chennai. The agency would find a number of patients for her, and then Dr. Murthy and her team would stage a one-day registration camp in that city. She would set up in a local school, meeting and examining patients and giving them appointments for their surgeries in Chennai. The registration camps had been a revelation to Dr. Murthy. She discovered that there were hundreds of patients who needed this surgery in the rural areas; they just had no idea that help was available. At her last camp, 120 patients and their families had waited in line to be examined. Dr. Murthy described watching the faces of the children as they congregated for the camp. The children with clefts stared at the other children with clefts. No one could believe it. Back in their villages, they had always been the only one.

It wasn't unusual for Dr. Murthy to operate on older children who had lived with the defect for many years. She told us about one of these, a fourteen-year-old boy called Davamurugan, from a small village 500km from Chennai. The boy was gangly with a mop of dark black hair and a very pronounced bilateral cleft—his upper lip was split twice, directly under each nostril, with the remaining middle section of his lip hanging uselessly from the base of his nose. He had the saddest expression in his eyes that Dr. Murthy had ever seen.

Davamurugan's parents confessed to the doctor that they had been so horrified when they first saw their newborn son that considered ending his life. Neither of them could bring themselves to hurt him, though, and so they tried to feed him, persisting even though the milk immediately leaked from the two holes in his lip. The boy's relatives refused to look at the baby or to touch him. When she went out on the street, the mother covered her baby with a sari—and even so, people turned away; they had heard that the family's new baby was a demon. When Davamurugan was old enough to go to school, his parents were determined that he would get an education. Even though he was constantly bullied, and the teachers refused to give him any attention in class, Davamurugan kept going back to school. He lagged far behind his classmates in his studies and at fourteen years old, he didn't have any friends. His parents continued to suffer alongside their son. They were terrified for his future.

For fourteen years, this family had thought that there was nothing anyone could do for Davamurugan. They had no idea that the boy's deformity was a defect and that it could be fixed. No one had ever told them—not the midwife, not the local health workers, not the boy's schoolteachers. No one knew. For fourteen years, they thought this was their lot. "The day we were told about your registration camp, we regained our lives back," the father told Dr. Murthy.

On the date of the appointment, the family came to Chennai by bus. Davamurugan was prepped for his surgery, and Dr. Murthy operated on his. The surgery was a complete success. Davamurugan had been living with his defect for 14 years, and now, after a 45 minutes surgery, he could go back home and start his life again.

"No one should have to wait 14 years for a surgery that takes 45 minutes," Dr. Murthy told the press. "This is our mission. To make certain that every child in our region with a cleft is helped."

When we began our partnership with Sri Ramachandra, Dr. Murthy had been convinced that it was going to difficult for her to find 500 patients to fulfill her quota.

A year later, together with her team, she had operated on 780 patients. No one was more surprised and more delighted than Dr. Jyotsna Murthy.

That first year, she told us, she learned something important.

"Our job isn't only to operate on these patients," she told us later. "It's to educate the population to let them know that surgery is available, that it is free and that this is a defect and that it can and will be fixed."

Dr. Murthy had plans to work with the government agencies, with local health worker and midwives, to enlist them in the work of informing families. She wanted to do more camps, going deeper and deeper into the rural areas. In all my years in business I had never met anyone who spoke with as much conviction as this doctor, highly qualified plastic surgeon could have left India and worked in Europe or America, like so many of her colleagues, making a lot more money and working a lot less hours. And yet she had chosen to stay here, where she felt she was needed. That day I didn't doubt she'd achieve anything she set her mind to.

From Chennai we headed south to Thrissur, in the state of Kerala, home of the Jubilee Mission Hospital, known locally as the "Poor Man's Hospital." Patients have been receiving treatment at Jubilee, regardless of their ability to pay, for over 50 years. Dr. Hirji Adenwalla, founder of The Charles Pinto Center for Cleft Lip and Palate at the hospital, was waiting to meet us on the porch of his small cottage in the hospital compound. He was in his seventies, spry and balding, with half-moon glasses on his nose. His wife Gulnar—tall and graceful, with cropped white hair—led us into a small dining room with a table set for tea.

There were two other guests at the tea party that day. One was an elderly New Zealander lady, wearing a dark red sari and glasses. She was introduced as Miss Phyllis Treasure. Dr. Adenwalla explained to us that Miss Treasure had come to Kerala in 1957 to run the Rehoboth Orphanage for girls in Thrissur, home to over 80 children.

Miss Treasure refused to call her establishment an orphanage, though.

"My children aren't orphans," she corrected the doctor gently. "They're my children. And I'm their mother."

The other guest at the table was one of Miss Treasure's children, a five-year-old Indian girl named Molly.

Molly was dressed for the occasion in a pale pink dress, her hair cut short and tied with a bow. There was no doubt that she was a beautiful child, but there was also something formidable about this tiny person. She had fire in her eyes. She looked across at us with a look of suspicion mixed with curiosity, ate her slice of cake, then she climbed down from the table and went out to explore the back yard.

Dr. Adenwalla took the opportunity to tell us her story.

"Let me tell you about Molly," he began. "She is a fighter. She never gives up. You see, Molly was born with a cleft lip." Soon after Molly was born, Dr. Adenwalla told us, she was poisoned—either by her parents or another family member—and left out on the streets to die. The person who had done this to Molly would have had no idea that her deformity was a birth defect. All this terrified person knew was that the baby was cursed, and that ending her life was better than subjecting her to a life with no future at all.

When a passerby found the infant, she was still breathing. She was taken to the local police station. The police said, "We don't look after babies. Take her to Dr. Adenwalla. Maybe he can do something for her."

"So they brought Molly to me," Dr. Adenwalla remembered. "I pumped the poison from her stomach and revived her. Then I called Miss Treasure, who said she would take her in. A few months later, when Molly was old enough, we operated on her, and repaired her cleft lip. Now, you can see, five years later, she had grown to be this beautiful little girl. And she is a survivor."

We asked Miss Treasure about how Molly was getting along. She was just starting school; she was learning to read. Miss Treasure told us that Molly liked to help with the younger children at Rehoboth. She was a hard worker. When Molly returned to the table, I noticed, for the first time, the faintest scar on her upper lip. Beyond that, it was impossible to guess what Molly had endured in her first few days in the world. She looked like any other healthy, inquisitive five-year-old. It was terrifying to think that she had almost died because no one knew that she could be helped.

That afternoon, we learned that Dr. Adenwalla and his wife had been living here at Jubilee Hospital, helping children like Molly, for over forty years. They had both been born in Bombay, to well-to-do Indian families. When they married, Dr. Adenwalla was working as a registrar at a prominent Bombay children's hospital, but he was convinced that his vocation lay elsewhere. He decided he wanted to leave India to become a medical missionary in Africa. He wanted to help the poor. He wanted to feel that he was living a life of meaning and purpose. Gulnar agreed to go with him. The only problem was, her parents were unhappy.

"You can go to Africa if you wish," Gulnar's father told him, "but you cannot take my daughter with you."

By now, Dr. Adenwalla was too much in love to leave without Gulnar, and so he resigned himself to staying in Bombay.

It was a cousin who pointed out to him that if he really wanted to help the poor, there were plenty of opportunities right here in India.

"Why do you need to go to Africa, when there are people who need you at home?"

This was how the newlyweds had come to live in Thrissur. Gulnar had seen an advertisement for a small mission hospital looking for a doctor. Dr. Adenwalla applied and was accepted. In 1961 when they arrived, the hospital was little more than a dispensary. It had fifteen beds, a rudimentary theatre, two nurses, and only two patients. But as the days and weeks progressed, it was clear that the Adenwallas had come to the right place. The community was in desperate need of a doctor, and in those early days, Dr. Adenwalla learned to wear many hats. He did all his own lab work. He had no radiologist, so he took his own x-rays. Without an anesthesiologist, he trained Gulnar to provide the necessary anesthesia in order to perform surgeries. He was delivering babies, setting fractures, performing C-sections and thoracic surgeries, tending to every kind of medical problem imaginable, from hernias to head injuries.

"I was the only doctor at Jubilee in those days," he smiled. "I would begin work at seven in the morning, and arrive home at one in the morning. At the end of a day like that, yes, you feel tired, but you feel a sense of achievement that sustains you into the next day." Gulnar remembered that their living conditions were far from ideal.

"The house had no running water—we had to draw water from the well—and we had one table fan which we would carry around with us from room to room to try and stay cool. But we were young and in love. It was an adventure."

Meanwhile, the couple's family and friends in Bombay were convinced that they had lost their minds. Why would they choose to live in such conditions when Dr. Adenwalla could be working at a nice hospital in Bombay? But the young doctor had been given something worth far more to him than material comfort: The Catholic Archdiocese of Thrissur who funded the hospital had given him the privilege of writing off any bill for any patient who was unable to pay.

"When you take away money from the business of being a doctor," the doctor explained, "when you are treating patients purely to help them, your reward becomes the gratitude of those you have helped. It becomes difficult to go back to any other way of working after you have experienced practicing medicine on these terms."

Over time, the hospital expanded and its facilities improved. In 1971, Jubilee Mission became recognized as a teaching hospital and could begin training doctors, which meant that Dr. Adenwalla was no longer working alone. With more surgeons on staff, he could start to specialize. By now, plastic and reconstructive surgery had become his obsession. His mentor in Bombay had been a man named Dr. Charles Pinto, a pediatric surgeon who had trained in plastic surgery after his own daughter was born with a cleft. It was Charles Pinto who taught Dr. Adenwalla the basic techniques of plastic surgery, at a time when this was still a relatively new specialty and there were very few plastic surgeons in India. Under the guidance of Pinto, Dr. Adenwalla began to focus on plastic and reconstructive surgeries, treating burns, performing skin grafts, fixing club feet, removing tumors, and of course, repairing clefts. But as much as Dr. Adenwalla loved the work, it was grueling. He was working long hours, on his feet all day, doing high volumes of surgeries. In 1994, when he was 64, he suffered a coronary. The year after that, he had a bypass. It was clear that he needed to begin scaling back.

At this point, he decided to focus on the surgery that brought him the most personal satisfaction: cleft repair. Dr. Adenwalla knew that there was very little money in clefts and almost no potential for recognition in the field. Instead, he chose clefts for a very simple reason: they made him happy.

"With no other surgery did I feel that I could have such an impact or create such a difference in the life of a patient," he told us. "In plastic surgery, you are constantly striving for perfection. The problem is, you always fall short of your expectations. A burn can be treated, and made to look better, but it can never be fully removed. An infected wound can be sealed with a skin graft, but the scar will never completely fade. But with cleft work, the results are dramatic and immediate and you know they will last for a lifetime."

Before partnering with Smile Train, Dr. Adenwalla had received a small amount of grant money from a Dutch charity and from the Church, but the rest he would have to raise himself as best he could. Despite such financial restrictions, in his forty-year career, he had already operated on 12,000 clefts. We could only imagine what he might accomplish with renewed funding and support.

After we finished our tea, we went to tour the hospital. It had come a long way since its early days as a dispensary. Nuns in their white saris bustled past, carrying meals for the patients in metal pails. A sign on a bulletin board read: "Fear not, for I am with thee." We learned that the hospital is still run by the local Catholic Diocese and yet the surrounding community that it serves is mostly Muslim. The Adenwallas are Zoroastrians, practicing one of the oldest monotheistic religions in the world. Strange bedfellows, and yet evidently, religious differences were unimportant here.

When Dr. Adenwalla walked into the cleft ward, everyone's eyes turned to him, nurses, mothers and children. He walked along the rows of neat metal beds. These were the patients who'd already received their surgeries and they had their arms wrapped in small splints and white bandages, so they wouldn't scratch at their stitches, making it look as if the ward were filled with children with broken arms. Dr. Adenwalla knew all their stories. Every mother had something she wanted to tell him, and he took as much time as necessary to speak to her and reassure her. His tone was soothing, his eyes were kind, he was completely focused on his patients, and they responded to him completely.

For most patients, the inflammation in the upper lip area was beginning to subside and the surgical wounds were already starting to heal. We saw mothers sitting by bedsides, gazing at their children. They knew that the "curse" had finally been lifted. They knew that they were returning home to start life again. I had never been in a ward with so many cleft patients before, an experience I'll never forget.

The head nurse was a nun in a white habit, the nurses were local girls in saris, and they were just as kindly and attentive as the doctor. They moved about the ward with quiet pride. They evidently revered the doctor and his wife, as if the Adenwallas set the pace for the ward and everyone else fell into step behind them. Dr. Adenwalla explained that many of these children would return for two or as many as five or six operations to correct their clefts in the most severe cases. This was the kind of continuity of care that was never going to be possible for doctors on medical missions, flying in and then leaving again.

After showing us the ward, Dr. Adenwalla took us to his operating room.

"Do you know what's the most important piece of equipment in an OR?" the doctor asked.

I shook my head.

"It's the light," he explained. "Without good light, a surgeon cannot perform his duties efficiently because he cannot see. The light makes the biggest difference to the outcome of the surgery. For forty years, I struggled with a third rate headlight—the contraption a plastic surgeon wears on his head when performing deep tissue work. I wore my eyes out without a decent light. Now along comes Smile Train and I have this beautiful, state-of-the-art headlight. My only regret now in life is that you didn't come along when I was a younger man!"

I calculated that Dr. Adenwalla must be in his early 70s. How much time did he have left to practice surgery? Another five, maybe ten years at the most. I wished we had come sooner. I wished we could have given him his light forty years ago.

When he'd finished showing us around, Dr. Adenwalla invited us back to his house for a nightcap before we went back to our hotel. Out on his porch, he poured us tumblers of his favorite single malt whiskey. We sat back in the velvet heat of the Indian night, swirling our drinks in our glasses.

I realized that I could hear what sounded like babies crying.

"What's that?" I asked.

"The children in the wards," Dr. Adenwalla said. I tried to put myself in the shoes of a man who, at the age of 70, would rather live next door to his patients than escape from the sound of them at the end of a long day. I knew that I could never be so good and I had never felt so humble.

"Doctor, you seem tireless," I told him. "What keeps you going?"

Dr. Adenwalla answered my question with another question:

"May I tell you a story?"

I nodded—of course.

"One afternoon not so long ago, a woman walked into my consulting room, carrying a little boy with a cleft. I could see from the scar on the mother's upper lip that she herself had a cleft, but that it had been repaired many years ago."

The doctor pointed out that it was extremely common for him to see a parent and child both with clefts as the defect has a genetic component.

"The woman put the child in my lap, and then she began sobbing," he went on. "She told me that her name was Bushara. She explained that she herself had been born with a cleft. She was her parent's fifth child. Her parents had loved her dearly and took her from hospital to hospital and doctor to doctor, trying to repair her deformity. She was given five operations, each of them more expensive, and more problematic than the last. Her father sold everything, their house, their farm, their belongings to get the money for her treatment. During this time, her mother died of TB. After this, Bushara's father became a worker on someone else's farm. Before long, the father died as well, broken-hearted. At 18, Bushara was married. Together with her husband, she had a small home and a small plot of land. They began to have children, four in a row, all of them healthy. Then her fifth child was born."

This was Mohammed, the baby sitting in Dr. Adenwalla's lap, the child with a cleft. "I was my father's fifth child," Bushara told Dr. Adenwalla. "'My cleft ruined his life. And so I made the decision that I would not let my fifth child ruin my family as I had ruined my family. I decided that I would never have my child operated upon. Never."

"This story was so touching to me," Dr. Adenwalla explained. "This woman had decided against the operation because of the financial cost. It was only when she heard about the free surgery that she came here for help. So you see why providing free cleft surgeries becomes a crusade. Every day I see young women arrive at the hospital with such a look of devastation and shame on their faces, hiding their children under their saris. Then, after the operation, the child is transformed. The stigma has gone. And the mother is transformed too. She leaves the hospital without shame, holding her child proudly and in daylight for the very first time."

I nodded again. This was what I had seen in China when I witnessed my first ever cleft surgery. It was this sense of transformation that was the reason for Smile Train, the reason I'd come here to India.

"But there is one last person who is changed by the surgery," Dr. Adenwalla went on. "This is the part you must understand. It is the surgeon himself who is transformed. A surgery like this is one of the most rewarding experiences in a surgeon's life. Every day, I see the smiles of mothers and children leaving the hospital. It's like throwing a smile into a pond, only to see ripples of smiles all over."

I was still new to the job back then. I thought Dr. Adenwalla and Dr. Murthy were exceptional, that we would never find doctors quite like them. I had no idea that wherever we went in the world, we would find surgeons devoting their lives to this cause, not for recognition or for money, but because they wanted to watch that ripple.

I lifted my glass, and proposed a toast: "To Dr. Adenwalla, the Mother Teresa of clefts!"

"Oh please," said Dr. Adenwalla, brushing off the compliment. "I don't believe that Mother Teresa ever had a taste for single malts…" With that, he raised his glass in my direction took another swig, and grinned.

.... NINE ....

Mr. Smile Train India

Our itinerary in India was ambitious: we were traveling from Chennai in the east down to Thrissur in the south west and from there east to Mangalore to Coimbatore in the south, then north to Bangalore and Mumbai. Each day we were up at five in the morning, on the go until ten at night, taking planes, trains, cars, and rickshaws. On the Indian roads, I held my breath until I was dizzy as our driver raced to overtake every car, bus, truck, or wandering cow in front of us. Just when I was sure that we were about to collide head-on with the vehicle directly ahead, we would swerve to safety again.

One afternoon, I finally got up the courage to speak.

"No disrespect sir," I said to our young driver. "You are clearly very good at your job because you always swerve at just the right time. But what if the oncoming driver is not as good a driver as you, what if he doesn't swerve in time? What if he is a bad driver?"

Our driver smiled and calmly told me, "Do not worry sir. In India, all the bad drivers are already dead."

I remember watching shirtless laborers carrying dirt on their heads at a construction site and asking our guide, "Where are all the bulldozers in India?"

"Why buy a machine when you can hire workers for 15 cents a day?" he replied.

These were parts of the world that had missed the Industrial Revolution altogether, not to mention the agricultural revolution. It was the first time I had ever seen people working in the fields, cutting crops with scythes, carrying the bales on their heads, raking and hoeing by hand.

I came back from India exhausted and exhilarated, but also thrown off balance. I'd never spent so much time with our partners in the field. I'd never visited so many hospitals. I'd lost count of how many patients and families I'd met on our trip; how many different dialects they'd spoken, the religions they practiced, all the many names of the cities, villages and hospitals we'd visited. In other words, the world looks very different at close quarters than it does from a distance. It's actually quite easy to make decisions on behalf of others when you're sitting in a nice office in midtown Manhattan. But it's a lot harder to know how to respond when you're experiencing firsthand a vast and diverse country that you've never visited before, where you don't speak the language, and you don't have any understanding of the culture. Before India, I was convinced that by applying my business 101 approach, I had all the answers. I had my spreadsheets, my PowerPoints, my charts, and projections. As we began the hard work of building up the Indian program from scratch, it was clear my education was just beginning.

Fortunately, I had a very good teacher: our country manager for India, Satish Kalra.

Satish had been guide throughout our travels in India. It was our country manager who woke us from our beds at dawn, dragged us half-sleeping into waiting cars, and who maintained our state of perpetual motion throughout our week long trip.

When Satish first heard about the position of country manager at Smile Train, he was on the verge of retirement after a long and successful career in business, at a crossroads in his life. He didn't enjoy golf and a consultancy job didn't appeal. His two grown daughters asked him, "Dad, why don't you do something that will make us proud?" When Satish told them he was thinking of going to work for Smile Train in India, they immediately said, "This is for you."

We'd given Satish the following brief: go ahead and create Smile Train India from scratch. It was a daunting proposal, but Satish was implacable. He had no prior non-profit experience and no medical experience when he came to Smile Train, but he had business acumen.

Satish had worked in senior management positions for major pharmaceutical companies all over the world. He was strategic, he was a problem-solver, and he was accustomed to tackling problems on a large scale. We had said we wanted to run Smile Train like a business, and Satish was business-minded to a fault. Our country manager was also budget-conscious, insisting on working from the spare bedroom of his apartment in Delhi rather than spending money on a separate office, laughingly calling himself 'the CEO and chief stamp licker of Smile Train India.' He was also an Indian in India. In the space of a year, this one man—working alone without any support staff—was responsible for increasing the numbers of cleft surgeries taking place in his homeland by 50%.

Despite his excellent credentials for the job, however, Satish was skeptical about what could be achieved in India in terms of numbers of surgeries. The reason was simple—he believed there were only a limited numbers of surgeons who were going to be willing to join the program.

"Clefts fall between the cracks," Satish explained. "Plastic surgeons do cosmetic procedures to pay their bills—nose jobs and so forth—and they do trauma and burns because those operations cannot wait. How do clefts fit into this equation? Clefts don't pay and these surgeries aren't emergency cases. There's no glory for a doctor providing cleft surgeries. Maybe there are a dozen other doctors in India who will be interested, but how we will persuade the rest?"

Satish already had found us a select group of hospitals with long-standing background in cleft work: Jubilee Mission, Sri Ramachandra, and five others included. Meanwhile, our aim was to deliver cleft surgeries to as many patients as we could, as rapidly as we could.

I felt Satish was holding us back.

Satish estimated that we would end up with 10 or 15 partner hospitals, doing 1000 surgeries a year, leveling off at somewhere around 5000 surgeries. I kept pressing him for more. A dozen hospitals would barely make a dent the backlog of one million clefts, let alone address new patients being born every day. We needed more partner hospitals. More surgeons. More surgeries. Satish came to meet with us at Smile Train's offices in New York. I remember demanding that he sign up more hospitals. Satish calmly explained to me that he wasn't going to do this. I ended up slamming my hand down on the table: "Let's make a real impact!" Satish told me he would never sacrifice quality for quantity. Looking back, I cringe. I was the fast, aggressive New Yorker, always pushing, staying on the offensive. Satish is a much more methodical, organized, and patient Indian, and he is also very good at standing his ground.

We continued this dance for some time, until at a certain point, we began to meet somewhere in the middle, a very good place to be. I conceded that Satish probably knew more about his own country than I did. And without ever completely adopting my simplistic credo of "more partners, more patients" our country manager did find us more partners and many, many more patients. Satish's strategy was to constantly working with our existing partners to figure out how they could become better and more effective in their work, and how Smile Train could support this. In his subtle but focused ways, Satish kept increasing our numbers of patients in India, year by year, and he did this by closely collaborating with partners to refine and expand the possibilities of their programs in ways I never could have dreamed up with in my faraway office in New York.

I had spent a week in India. Satish, meanwhile, spent every week in India, crisscrossing the country, communicating with partners on a daily basis.

In Varanasi, our country manager met with a young surgeon in the program, Dr. Jayanto Kumar Tapadar. Dr. Tapadar was in charge of a 30-bed reconstructive surgery unit at the Ramakrishna Mission Home of Service in the city. For the past ten years, this doctor had been providing free cleft lip and cleft palate surgeries to the local community, and his partnership with Smile Train meant he could afford to offer many more surgeries than ever before. Dr. Tapadar only had one complaint. Although our funding was enabling him to provide more surgeries, it was an ongoing challenge getting patients to actually come to his hospital.

"In terms of numbers, we haven't even scratched the surface," Dr. Tapadar told Satish.

Like Dr. Murthy our surgeon in Chennai, Dr. Tapadar was spending a few days each month, traveling out into the rural areas, staging camps where patients could be registered and examined before coming to the city for their surgeries. The problem was, often the patient wouldn't show up for the appointment.

Dr. Tapadar told the story of a family of three, all with unrepaired clefts, a mother, father and their little boy, who had come to one of his registration camps. The father refused to have the surgery—he said it was too late for him. The mother was pregnant, so her surgery could wait until after she had the child. But Dr. Tapadar gave the family and date and time for a surgery for the little boy. To his dismay, the day of the appointment came and went. The family never made it to Varanasi.

When Dr. Tapadar contacted the local health worker who had arranged the camp about the missing patients, he heard the same reason he had heard many times. The families couldn't afford the travel fare. They lived over 400km from Varanasi. The cost of the bus fare was only a few rupees, yet it was prohibitive for a family living from hand to mouth. For Dr. Tapadar, this was the hardest part of his work—knowing that patients needed these surgeries, but that because of lack of funds, they couldn't reach him.

"I only wish I had a fairy godmother who could deliver these patients to me," Dr. Tapadar told Satish.

Later that day, while he was traveling home to Delhi, Satish thought to himself, "Well, maybe we don't need a fairy godmother; maybe we just need to reimburse patients for their travel costs." Soon afterwards, Smile Train India began offering small grants to our partner hospitals cover travel expenses. Patients were told that if they showed a receipt for their bus ticket or train ticket when they arrived at the hospital, they would be reimbursed immediately. After the travel grants were introduced, Dr. Tapadar went from operating on 233 patients in the previous year to 1871 patients the following year—an increase of over 1,500 patients.

Who would have thought that a few dollars to pay for bus fare could make such a dramatic difference? The cost to Smile Train had been extremely nominal and yet the results in terms of numbers have been extraordinary.

Satish uncovered another problem facing our surgeons. As their numbers of patients increased, it followed that they needed more time in the operating room. In a busy hospital, emergency surgeries always come first, and it is an article of faith with Smile Train that we would never divert resources or operating room time away from patients in greater need. At one hospital in Lucknow, Satish discovered that there were three plastic surgeons in the hospital, but that the only window when they could use the operating room was on Saturday for half a day. When Smile Train built a dedicated operating room in Lucknow and opened it for business, output increased and the facilities were improved for all patients at the hospital.

As numbers in India continued to grow, even as his boss in New York continued to press him for "more, more, more" Satish became increasingly focused on improving the quality of the experience for the patient.

"What else do your families need?" he asked our partners.

"So many of our families struggle to feed their children," Dr. Tapadar told Satish. "I'd like to have cooking oil and pulses to send home with them, so they have enough to feed the baby while that child is recovering from surgery."

"We always say that a child can go to school after cleft surgery," Dr. Ravi Kumar Mahajan, from Amritsar, pointed out. "But many of our children don't have the money for school registration fees. I'd like to send them home with money for that."

"Children with clefts often have such low self-esteem, especially those who have lived with their deformities for a number of years. We want to buy the children a new dress or pair of pants, so that they return home feeling proud of themselves."

This suggestion came from Dr. Atul Sharma, at his hospital in Hissar.

"We want to buy toys for these children who have never owned a doll or a toy train in their lives," explained Dr. Asif Masood, from Gorakhpur. "They've suffered so much at such a young age. They deserve to have something that puts a smile on their faces."

Satish called these new grants "Smile Grants" and their stated purpose was to put a smile on the patient's face beyond the surgery itself. The average amount of these stipends is equivalent to $20 and yet a small amount can make a huge difference. Satish understood that Smile Train could never manage to completely rehabilitate children living in poverty—but that if we could help children to smile after their surgeries, then that was well within our mission. Smile Grants are now used in our partner hospitals all over the world where every partner hospital finds its own way of using the money. In the Philippines, Dr. Michelle Aportadera gives the children an ice cream after their surgeries: in part because it helps to numb a sore lip, but also because, for most of these children, it's the first ever taste of ice-cream. She would rather see that expression of delight on their faces as they take that first bite, the doctor tells us, than the seven wonders of the world.

Satish himself recently had a powerful reminder of the function of these grants. He was crossing the street while visiting one of our partners in Varansi, when he happened to notice a rickshaw driver ahead of him with an unrepaired cleft. While the man was stopped at some lights, Satish took the opportunity to find out why it hadn't been fixed.

"Don't you know?" he asked the rickshaw driver. "You can have your cleft repaired free of charge at a hospital near here?"

"Yes, I know," the man replied. Satish was confused.

This man was living and working in Varanasi. He could travel to the hospital in his rickshaw.

"So why don't you go?" Satish asked.

"If I go for the surgery, they say I will have to stay there five days. I drive this rickshaw during the day and my family eats at night. I can't lose five days of work; my family will starve."

"How much do you earn?" Satish immediately asked.

The man told him the amount, which was equivalent to $2 a day. Satish gave him $20 and scribbled down the address of the nearest Smile Train partner hospital. "Go tomorrow. Go get your surgery. Please."

After Satish handed the man the address and the money, the rickshaw driver stood in the middle of the street as the lights, and the cars moved all around him. He was staring at the piece of paper. He had started to cry.

By now, a small crowd had gathered around to see what was going on. Even the passenger in the back of the rickshaw climbed out of the cab to find out what the fuss was about. But instead of shouting at the driving for holding up the journey, the passenger gave the rickshaw driver a hug. He told him, "Come on, you're going to be okay. You can drop me off, and then you can go and get your surgery. "

This man had lived with his cleft for more than twenty years. Now, because of a chance meeting, he could finally receive the surgery he should have received as his birthright.

As I write this, we have eight local country managers and regional directors working across the developing world—in Africa, China, Latin America, South Asia, South East Asia, and Russia—and like Satish, each of them is our eyes and ears on the ground. They work with our partners to improve the quality of the experience of our patients, and to remove whatever barriers stand in the way of a patient receiving the care that he needs. It's relentless and essential work that none of us in New York are able to do from this great distance.

Back in 2001, Satish had been convinced that we'd never break more than 5,000 surgeries. Nearly ten years down the road, we have completed 260,000 surgeries in India. We were a long way from fully addressing a backlog of a million unreparied clefts, but we have put a foot on the mountain. In this respect, the credit goes—not to an impatient American in his office in New York, slamming his hand on the table—but to a group of devoted doctors, and an ingenious and stubborn local manager, with his ear very close to the ground, who taught me that sometimes, if you stop pushing, and start listening, you can get a lot more done.

.... TEN ....

The Bright Spot

In 1998, a couple called Dr. Andrew and Sarah Hodges from the UK were based at a church mission hospital in Uganda when they began to recognize the extent of the cleft problem throughout this African nation. They had the idea to write to every hospital in Uganda, asking if they could visit to repair clefts. Andrew is a surgeon; Sarah is an anesthesiologist.

When the couple would arrive at a hospital, more often than not, the staff would tell them, "There are no cleft patients here." But as soon as word got out that free surgeries were available, patients would start to appear. Parents of children suffering with this defect were so ashamed and persecuted that they were keeping their sons and daughters hidden. Until now, the hospital staff had no idea these children existed.

Over a period of eight months, the Hodges visited twenty hospitals across the country, treating 30, 40, sometimes as many as 60 patients for every trip. These hospitals were in remote and rural areas, often without running water or adequate electricity. When the electricity generators failed—which they often did—the Hodge's back-up light consisted of two Land Rover headlamps attached to a battery.

But by the end of the eight months the Hodges had completed in 377 surgeries. This wasn't all they had accomplished. They had literally kick-started cleft care in Uganda, a place when an estimated 1,100 babies are born with clefts each year, 100% of which at that time were going unrepaired.

When Andrew first wrote to us, it was the year 2000. He had since left Uganda and he was completing his training as a plastic surgeon in England. Now he wanted to go back to Uganda with Sarah to stage more missions, traveling around the country to operate on clefts again.

Our response to this request showed the degree of our naivety about the challenges that lay ahead for us.

"No, we're sorry," we told Andrew. "We don't fund Western doctors who want to do mission work. We train and empower local doctors doing cleft work in their own countries." Andrew wrote back to us and told us—respectfully—that as far as he knew, there was not a single surgeon operating on clefts anywhere in Uganda, a country with a population of 12 million people.

We felt had to stick to our guns. We didn't fund missions. It was only when the Hodges returned to Uganda in 2004—at which point they would be permanently based in the country—that we officially began our partnership with them. As we got to know Andrew and Sarah better, the couple lobbied hard for us to change some of the terms on which our partner grants were based. The Hodges wanted to get out into the field, going on missions around Uganda with their traveling kit, and they wanted us to fund them. Meanwhile, we felt strongly that the Hodges needed to do their surgeries and training exclusively at Mengo. The Hodges pointed out that in a country with zero awareness about clefts and with a population spread out over many hundreds of kilometers, where children are hidden in their homes from shame, it was going to be difficult, in fact impossible, to reach remote communities without going to them directly. But this was the model that we had used in China and in India. It was a model that we felt was working. We wanted to the patients to come to the doctors, not the other way around.

DeLois and I were determined to figure out some way to help the Hodges extend their reach, while encouraging them to stay at their base in Kampala. We held the purse strings and we thought we knew best. This was our first partner in any African country and at that point, we were still convinced that all we had to do was apply our model in its present form to succeed wherever we went in the world. We felt that if surgeries were taking place in a bigger, better equipped urban hospital, we could maintain a higher degree of quality control. As the saying goes, when all you have is a hammer, everything looks like a nail.

Sadly, we hadn't even begun to fully appreciate the severe limits of existing medical provision in Uganda. The World Health Organization consistently ranks the country's healthcare performance as one of worst in the world. Average life expectancy here is 42 years old and maternal mortality is amongst the highest anywhere—one in every 200 births ends the mother's life. This is a country where one million people are living with HIV and where malaria accounts for 14% of all deaths—meanwhile, only 10% of children under five are sleeping under an insecticide-treated mosquito net. In 2005, the year of our visit, the shortage of doctors, surgeons, and medical workers was at chronic proportions, with more than half of all healthcare positions in Uganda going unfilled. It was this vast disparity between need and provision that had motivated the Hodges to come here in the first place.

In 2005, we set out to visit the Hodges at Mengo Hospital in Kampala. The first time we met the couple, they were standing outside the entrance to the outpatient unit in the bright blazing sun. My immediate thought was that they looked like fishes out of water, a whiter than white English couple in the middle of this teeming, African city. Right away, they introduced us to their children, two boys and their daughter Rachel, the Ugandan girl they'd adopted in 1997. Rachel, we later learned, had a cleft which Andrew had repaired after she was abandoned as a baby.

As we walked through a small door into the hospital, the Hodges pointed out a portrait of the hospital's founder, a British man named Sir Albert Cook, a medical missionary had come to Uganda over a century ago, and who was exceptional amongst missionaries at that time in that he pioneered the training of local doctors and medical workers. Mengo Hospital is the oldest hospital in East Africa, and although it has since moved to much larger, newer premises, in 2006 when we visited, it was still housed in the small facility that Sir Albert had established over a hundred years ago. Although The Christian Blind Mission was doing its best to repair the place and patch it up, the facility was woefully small. Ahead of us were two tiny operating rooms, abutting an even narrower recovery room. Space and time was at such a premium here that the doctors had to sterilize equipment in the same room they ate lunch, so that they wouldn't have to leave their patients. The operating room was so cramped that the oxygen cylinder that supplied the anesthetic machine had to be kept outside, with a tube threaded through an open window. When the supply ran low, someone had to run to get outside to change it.

The Hodges led us through a long, thin general ward, with beds on either side. We passed patients with malaria, pneumonia, and every variety of surgical condition. Drip bottles were hanging from nails in the wall; mosquito nets were draped over every bed, each of which was filled. At the end of the long ward was another door.

"This is our ward," said Andrew.

Inside the small room, there were eight beds, all of different heights and sizes, each one squeezed in beside the next one. The Hodges shared this minuscule unit with an orthopedic surgeon. In one bed, a boy had large metal fixators attached his fractured arms and legs after an accident; another boy, even younger, had an arm had been amputated due to a bone infection. Andrew's patients included a girl who had been terribly burned after falling into a cooking fire—the majority of Ugandans cook on open fires—but until now her burns had gone untreated. This little girl's forefinger had been attached to her thumb by scar tissue—now she was going to be able to feed herself, dress herself, and hold a pencil. Then, in the single crib at the back of the ward, Andrew showed us an eight-month baby who was so malnourished because of the cleft in her palate that he weighed only seven pounds (a healthy baby should weigh 20 pounds at that age). The Hodges' son, Sam, just ten years old, tenderly placed his hand on the boy's stomach—his hand was bigger than this baby's entire torso. Andrew was trying to help the baby gain weight, so that he could eventually operate on him.

After we finished our tour of the outpatient unit, the Hodges took us to the hospital's rehabilitation clinic, a short drive away, at a separate facility, where they saw their patients before surgery and where patients could be sent to recover if there wasn't enough room for them in the ward. Again, this clinic was shared with the orthopedic department. Here we met a two-year-old boy with both legs gone from the thigh down due to an infection. Another child was in a wheelchair—both of his legs were in casts after a horrifying fall. In a room behind the dormitory, there was a workshop for making prostheses, wheelchairs, braces, and splints for the children. We saw a man stripping old bicycles to make parts for makeshift wheelchairs for children with polio and spina bifida. Then, I noticed what I thought was a pile of little baseball bats. Andrew explained that these were prostheses for children whose legs had been amputated, either due to a bone infection or landmine trauma. So many! The sight of that pile of tiny plastic legs was one of the most depressing things I've ever seen.

Despite such compromised facilities and an overwhelming need, the Hodges and their colleagues were helping children who otherwise would have had no where else to turn. Sadly, a child with a disability in a country lacking basic medical resources goes to the bottom of every list. That day, we met two surgeons from Italy. Like Andrew and Sarah, they had made a home for themselves in Uganda. We met Ugandan nurses, social workers, and anesthetic officers (medical workers who can administer local anesthetic), all devoted to their work. We also met a trainee surgeon from Kampala called Dr. George Galiwango, whom Andrew was working with. Three year's after our visit, George would pass his regional plastic surgery exams, and he continues to perform cleft surgeries for Smile Train to this day.

Now that Andrew had shown us the facility at Mengo, he wanted to take us "upcountry" to visit a hospital called Kumi in a remote part of Northern Uganda, so we could see his work outside the city. The following day, we took off from a small airstrip on the outskirts of Kampala, traveling in a small four-seater plane. By car, the journey to Kumi would take six hours across bone-jarring dirt roads—many of them close to impassable—but by plane we could get there in a little over an hour. Andrew was training to become a licensed pilot so he could fly upcountry to reach otherwise hard-to-access communities. We took off at dawn, crossing Lake Victoria, following the course of the Nile alongside flat swamplands that were the most intense green. When you think of Africa, you expect dry, parched scrubland, but there was something unexpectedly lush about the Ugandan landscape, with its bright blue water and vivid grasslands. About an hour later, Kumi airstrip was in sight—a grass runway that the pilot had to buzz first to scare away any animals. Then he had to circle steeply back in order to land before the animals returned. With a series of gigantic and terrifying bumps—and a lot of swerving to avoid rocks on the runway—we finally landed.

Kumi Hospital is a former leprosy hospital, founded in 1927 by the Church Missionary Society. In 1985, during the period of regime change in Uganda, war broke out and the hospital was all but destroyed. Infrastructure and services collapsed, and the farm on which the hospital depending for its livelihood was looted and decimated. In 1997, the hospital became a general hospital, but the conditions here were still desperate. Andrew explained to us that Kumi Hospital was suffering from the same problems faced by so many rural hospitals in Uganda. There wasn't enough money to pay staff, and so the hospital was continually losing its nurses and doctors to other hospitals and NGOs in urban areas. Without nurses, families were left to look after the patients themselves. All around the hospital, people were squatting in makeshift tents, around outdoor fires, while they waited for family members to recover. This hospital had no gynecologist, no pediatrician, no anesthesiologist, and certainly no plastic surgeon. But despite such impossible challenges, the hospital superintendent, Dr. John Opolot—a dead ringer for Dr. Martin Luther King—was upbeat and enthusiastic. As he took us around, he would describe the difficulties he was facing before repeating the same words, "Things are looking up..."

Every morning, Dr. Opolot and his tiny staff would begin the day with a prayer service. Their faith kept them going, he told us. I had a strong sense that I was meeting with a saint. This man was doing everything he could, but he was the first to admit he didn't have the skilled staff necessary to deal even with basic medical work, let alone reconstructive surgery cases. It was clear that Dr. Opolot was extremely happy to have an outside doctor like Andrew visiting his hospital to conduct surgeries. In fact, he deemed it vital.

"Without Andrew, we would be unable to treat hundreds of our patients," he explained.

Inside the hospital, the surgical ward was jammed. Patients were sleeping two in a bed, some patients even sleeping on the floor. The room was so dark I wondered how the nurses could find the patients, until I remembered that almost no nurses here.

After our visit to Kumi, Andrew had arranged to take us around some of the local villages, to meet patients he had already operated on through his work at Kumi. A social worker named Charles had spent the previous week riding through the villages on his bicycle seeking out these patients in their homes. Together with Charles and Andrew, we now set off in a rickety old Range Rover, driving along ferociously bumpy dirt roads. After a while, I realized that ours was the only car. Everyone else was walking, usually barefoot, the men carting machetes on their backs, and the women carrying logs and dried brush on their heads. We passed by field after field where hundreds of people in rags were hunched over, hacking in the soil with backhoes, scattering seeds and cutting wheat by hand. There were no oxen, donkeys or horses. Apart from a few goats, there was no livestock. No tractors. No irrigation. The local agriculture was almost Stone Age. Looking out the window of our jeep, it occurred to me that our pilgrims in Plymouth, Massachusetts almost 400 years ago had more equipment and resources than this destitute part of the world.

"Flying in surgeons to places like Kumi is the only way to help these children," Andrew insisted. "Travel to Kampala is an impossible prospect for families living in these areas. They're too poor and afraid to even think of making the trip to the big city."

We learned that rural Uganda is divided up into tribal areas along strict lines—many people spend their whole lives without going much further than their own village. There are 40 different languages here, and if you leave your area, you might not be able to communicate, let alone figure out the public transport system and find your way in a major city you've never visited before.

"At Kumi, I can do twenty clefts in two days," Andrew went on. "Charles finds me the patients and I can operate on them at Kumi, which is very close to their homes. I've been in situations up here where I've begged parents with a malnourished child to come to Kampala for treatment because it will be safer to operate there. I've told them, your child is going to die unless you go to the capital. They say, well, my child is going to die, and they go back to the village. They're too scared, too poor, too intimidated to make the journey."

In one of the villages we met Ajok. The 10-year old girl did her best to smile for the camera, but she was still healing from her surgery. Huddled in a corner of her one-room grass and mud hut were three of the girl's four younger brothers. Like so many families, a $1.60 mosquito net was a luxury they could not afford. Every night before bedtime they would light a fire to create enough smoke to keep the mosquitoes at bay. But, by 2 a.m., while they were sleeping, the fire would go out and the insects would come pouring in. Without a mosquito net, the chances of the children contracting malaria were extremely high.

The girl's father, a farm laborer, had died six months earlier from AIDS, whereupon the family lost their sole source of income. They showed me the grave where their father was buried, right next to their hut. It had a cross and a little inscription written on a stone, and they had placed his old hat on top of it. I tried to imagine these children walking past that stone and their father's hat every day. The mother, who was 35, looked about 60. Chances were high that she had AIDS too. How long did she have to live? Who was going to look after these children if she didn't survive?

As I snapped my photos, that mother stared at me with hard eyes. "All you want is to come and take photos, and then you'll leave." This was how I had interpreted her stare. And she was right. Her daughter had received the surgery, but that wasn't going to save this family from malaria and starvation. It took everything I had to set my face into a smile. I didn't want this little girl to see the full horror of her situation reflected in my eyes.

I crouched down to her level, shook her hand and asked, "What's your name?"

"Ajok," she mumbled. Dr. Hodges explained to us that most female children in this area born with clefts are called Ajok. The boys are called Ojok. The Hodges told us that when he looked at his patient list for cleft surgeries, the majority of his patients had this same name.

"It means, 'cursed by God,'" Charles explained.

Many patients change their names after their operations, but this girl was still Ajok, the name she'd had all her life. Maybe at some point, she would get a new name, but in many ways her life would still be cursed. Andrew's surgery had repaired this little girl's cleft, but the way ahead was still unimaginably hard.

The trip upcountry troubled me, and for reasons I could have never predicted. Before we left for our visit to Uganda, one of the members of our advisory board had asked me: "Why are you bothering with Africa?" he'd said. "Think about all the problems there: malaria, inadequate water supply, wars, famine, HIV and AIDS. Fixing clefts is a drop in the bucket. Who cares about clefts when so many people are dying?"

I had heard this argument before in one form or another since the earliest days of The Smile Train, from local government officials, from health workers, from doctors themselves. "Clefts are a cosmetic problem," they would say; "they're not an emergency"; "you can't expect local doctors to prioritize clefts over the important work of saving lives." Although I saw the reasoning behind this attitude, I couldn't agree with it. What was the answer? Ignore the problem of clefts exists altogether? Turn our heads away because it's too much of a challenge? Yes, there are more pressing problems facing mankind and we're the first to acknowledge we're too small of an organization to solve all of them. Our focus is clefts because we see this is a real and meaningful way to have an impact on the life of a child.

But now I didn't feel so sure.

Were we doing the right thing? Maybe my friend in New York was right. Ajok and her family were facing so many problems, AIDS, malaria, malnutrition. Were we right to be prioritizing clefts here?

Andrew shook his head, sadly.

"It is hard," he told us. "We've been trying to track the children we treated last year, and we've already discovered that five of them have died of malaria.

This has nothing to do with the cleft operation. It has everything to do with being a child in Africa. We send them home healthy, and a few months later, they get malaria. But..." Andrew paused, taking his glasses off and rubbing them with shirt, as if giving himself time to put how he felt into words. "But this doesn't mean we should be doing these surgeries. No one else is tackling the problem of clefts, or of children with defects and disabilities in general. For me, this is all the more reason to treat them. This is the work we should be doing at a mission hospital like Mengo. These children deserve medical attention just as much anyone else. Yes, there are bigger issues in Africa. But with clefts, we can see the profound impact of the surgery on the individual, and I believe that counts for an enormous amount.

That evening, we had dinner with Andrew's students, young Ugandan doctors who were committed to staying in Uganda and helping their fellow countrymen. They were an impressive bunch. Smart, educated and totally committed to making a difference. They cared about their country a lot and he cared about the people—but they explained to me that the government has too many other priorities to devote money or resources to specialized medical training. "We can train in general surgery," they explained, "but it is much more challenging to find a way of training in a specialty when there are no government funded opportunities." This was how they had come her to work with Andrew. DeLois and I left feeling hopeful, but still concerned about the conditions we had seen on our trip upcountry. These just didn't seem like a safe environment in which to conduct surgeries.

After Uganda, we flew to Nairobi, Kenya to meet another one of our partners. But this time, we weren't visiting a hospital. We were going to the offices of AMREF, the African Medical Research Foundation That day, we met Dr. Asrat Mengiste, a surgeon with the organization. Born in Addis Ababa, Asrat was one of the surgeons operating on clefts in the whole of Ethiopia—a nation with a population of 80 million. We were meeting Asrat at the organizations offices, rather than a hospital, was because he didn't work from a hospital. Instead, he spent his weeks traveling to remote rural hospitals throughout East Africa, visiting small hospitals, operating on patients who need reconstructive surgeries, and training local surgeons to eventually do this work for themselves.

Again, we voiced our concerns. What were these hospitals like? What were the facilities like? Why can't you bring patients to Addis Ababa for treatment?

With great restraint, Asrat answered us.

"Yes, the hospitals facilities are compromised by most standards," he told us. "The challenges of performing surgery in these hospitals are immense. Water supplies are often limited, surgical facilities and basic medical equipment are poor or even non-existent. Power cuts happen all the time. But for a local patient living in one of these areas, these missions are their only hope."

Asrat told us about a recent visit to a hospital in Arbarmich, a small town 500km south of Addis Ababa. Here he met a 35-year-old woman with a three-year-old child. Both of them had cleft lips. This woman grew up believing that she was cursed and she was terrified that her child would suffer just as she had done. She never went to school. She spent her childhood at home, cooking for her family, collecting firewood and fetching water. It is only after she was married that she learned about the surgery for her condition—but she was told it was available only in the capital city, Addis Ababa.

"In order to get to Addis, this woman would have to travel 500 kilometers," Asrat explained. "This would take many days. She didn't have the money for transportation. She spoke a different dialect and knew she would be unable communicate even if she could reach Addis. She desperately wanted her child to have the surgery, and yet she had no way to help him."

"We would never had been able to help this patient if we stayed in Addis Ababa," Asrat reiterated. "The rural areas are where the vast majority of our patients live. I'm telling you, if we don't go to them, we won't be able to treat them." Asrat was someone immensely qualified, committed and proud of his work helping his own people. We left that day impressed but still hanging onto our conviction that we couldn't compromise our standards.

Later that day, however, we met with an official from the Kenyan Ministry of Health to talk about the Smile Train program. Like so many people we met on our visit, he was relieved to hear that we were working with local partners.

"You know, people from the West are always coming here and telling us what we should be doing," the official explained. "The problem is that as a result, we only receive grants for the things that the West wants to see. For instance, we get lots of grants to build schools because donors like to see pictures of schools in their brochures. When you have pictures of schools in your brochures, it's easy to raise money because people feel good about building schools. So we have more schools than we need! But no one is interested in paying for teachers! We have such a shortage of teachers here that the average number of students in a classroom is 90. If you point this out to an organization that builds schools, they tell you, sorry, we're only interested in building schools."

His words have stayed with me ever since.

After we came back to New York, we told our African partners we were committed to helping fund their missions to remote hospitals like Kumi and Arbamich. How could we in good conscience do otherwise? Personally, I was on an extremely steep learning curve with our new African partners, but I knew enough to understand that I had to keep asking questions and listening to answers. Millions of dollars of aid from the West have poured into Africa over the past thirty years. And yet so many grand plans have failed. I'd seen with my own eyes, children living in a house filled with smoke because her family didn't have a mosquito net to protect her. Schools are built without people to staff them. Without feedback from the people you're helping, how could you ever assume that you know what they need from you? We couldn't impose all the solutions from the top down. We had to adapt to real life in these communities, and work from the bottom up. By listening to the surgeons, to the managers, to the families, by respecting our partners, by not dictating, we felt that we could inch closer to our goal.

By June of 2010, we had 122 partners across 17 African nations, a mission groups that go into a further 11 countries. The vast majority of these surgeons are Africans helping Africans, incredible committed, devoted men and women who stay in their country, not for money or recognition, but because they feel it is the right thing to do. We continue to offer training opportunities for these doctors. We host symposiums, trainings, and conferences for them, inviting them to participate in training opportunities at home, and around the world. At one of these international symposiums, we met a surgeon from Ghana called Dr. Peter Donkor. He told us, "What we really need in Africa is a sense of pride, we need to be self-sufficient. We need our own cleft association, so that surgeons can share expertise and support each other." Based on this idea, we provided the funding to start the Pan African Cleft Lip Association. Every year since 2006, we've been hosting cleft medical symposiums that take place in Nigeria. More than 125 surgeons and medical professionals from 14 African countries attend for several days of training and professional development.

Since we visited Uganda in 2006, Andrew and Sarah have moved to a new facility for Mengo in Kampala. They now work transporting patients from the outlying areas, so they can treat them at their new facility in Mengo. Over a period of five years, Asrat and AMREF have gone from helping 150 patients with clefts to 1,500 patients with clefts each year, throughout East Africa. On each of his visits, Asrat works with the local medical staff, training them in cleft surgeries, so that many of local doctors now perform surgeries directly for Smile Train. One of these, Dr. Endale Berber, works at the same hospital in Arbaminch where Asrat visited and operated on the mother who had been waiting for her surgery for 35 years. Dr. Berber began performing cleft surgeries in 2010, the first surgeon at the hospital to do so, thanks to Asrat's training. Now, patients living in this area no longer have to wait for a flying doctor to visit, they can be operated on year round. Give time, things improve.

This past January, 2010, I attended a dinner in Ethiopia with our fifteen partner surgeons there, local surgeons, who perform over 600 surgeries for us every year. At the time of writing we are providing around 8,000 surgeries per year in Africa. It's an improvement (especially considering that our first year in Africa we operated on 370 patients) but it's not enough. For a continent with one billion people we should be helping 20,000 to 40,000 children a year. That's what we're aiming for, and we continue to stand by this work. Sadly, no one has yet truly figured out how to save the millions of children dying from malaria, TB, and AIDS. But there is a simple cure for clefts. It's one of the rare success stories. It's a small ray of hope, a bright spot, in a place where medical miracles can be few and far between.

.... ELEVEN ....

Things They Never Taught Me at Harvard

The beaten-up old ambulance clung to the curves of the road as the slope turned from tarmac to mud, and from mud to ice. Without guard rails, every hairpin turn seemed to take us closer to the precipice, making for a heart-pounding ride. Outside, it must have been twenty degrees, low enough to make us shudder inside our winter coats. Eventually, the road gave out altogether and we stopped at a small commune, made up of tiny, barren lots of land divided between the local peasants. The rest of the journey we made on foot, along a dirt path that took us higher into the hills. Ahead of us were cliffs the color of clay, patched with snow and scrub. This was Shanxi province in China, a bleak frontier on the border with Inner Mongolia. To a New Yorker, it felt like the ends of the earth. But by now, I had learned to bring less of an agenda, and more of an open mind to these journeys into the field. This time, I let the experience come right at me.

We were here with Dr. Liu Xinhua, our partner surgeon at the First People's Hospital of Jingzhou; just a few hours' drive from here. Dr. Xinhua grew up in these hills; he was born in Shanxi in 1955, the son of farmers. To look at him, you probably wouldn't guess he was a surgeon. Big shouldered and tall, with wild black hair, and a cigarette dangling from his mouth John Wayne-style, he gave the impression of a man who was probably just as comfortable riding a horse bareback as he would be with a scalpel in hand. When it came to helping children with clefts, however, there was no mistaking Dr. Xinhua's commitment. Every weekend—after five long days at the hospital—Dr. Xinhua would get behind the wheel of this former ambulance, to drive up into these hills, searching the countryside for children with clefts.

"When we were first starting out, we had so few patients coming to the hospital," Dr. Xinhua explained, speaking in Mandarin, with a thick local accent, our interpreter told us. "We knew that there were many more children who could benefit from the program. We just had to find them."

As a boy growing up in rural Shanxi, Dr. Xinhua could remember children in his own village with clefts.

"Everyone looked down on these children, on the whole family," he recalled. "Even though I was young, I remember thinking that this was wrong. No one asks to be born with a cleft. No parent wants a child to suffer. I thought that maybe if I could become a doctor, I could help these children to have normal lives."

Dr. Xinhua began his medical work in Jingzhou in 1977. He started specializing as a dental surgeon in 1983, developing a special interest in cleft lip and palate surgeries. When he was appointed director of the Dental Department at the First People's Hospital in Jingzhou—the year Smile Train began partnering with the hospital—this meant he could devote the majority of his time to treating clefts, the reason he had gone into his specialty in the first place. Beginning in 2001, he started building Smile Train cleft program at the hospital from the ground up.

Because he'd grown up in rural Shanxi, Dr. Xinhua knew that there were no shortage of children with clefts in the rural areas. It was lack of education and awareness—not lack of patients—that was the reason for the small numbers of surgeries he was completing in the beginning.

"Many families outside of the city have no idea that such surgery exists," Dr. Xinhua told us. "Even those who do, often doubt it can really be of any help to them."

And so Dr. Xinhua began spending his weekends on the road. He knocked on doors; he went to marketplaces, local health clinics and orphanages, handing out pamphlets He visited the most remote parts of the province, places that were impossible to reach with conventional advertising, because no one living there had access to televisions or newspapers. He met patients and their families face to face, persuading them to come to Jingzhu for the surgery. If these families couldn't afford the bus fare, he would pick them up and drive them to the hospital himself. His colleagues began to join him on these weekend trips. Shanxi province is about the size of the state of Florida, and yet in the space of four years, Dr. Xinhua and his team had already covered more than ninety counties and cities in the region. They would leave before dawn and return well into the night, living on instant noodles and bottled water.

Since 2001, they had gone from treating 50 patients a year to close to 500 patients each year.

Dr. Xinhua had brought us here because he wanted to introduce us to one of the families he'd met on his travels. He strode ahead of us, and we did our best to keep up, until we began to hear dogs baking and a whisper of smoke in the sky, sure signs of a village ahead. "This is Yu Village," the doctor told us.

It was only as we came closer that I realized that what I assumed were cliffs were actually terraces cut into the hillside, and that these terraces were pockmarked with windows and doors.

"These are the villagers' homes," our interpreter explained.

Those doorways were entrances to caves carved into the hillside. Dr. Xinhua and our interpreter explained to us that thousands of people in Shanxi live in caves like these, called yaodongs in the local dialect.

"They live here because they can't afford to go anywhere else," Dr. Xinhua said.

Clearly, I'd been spending too much time in Manhattan—I had no idea that there were people in the world who were still living in caves. Five thousands years of human history later, I had an ipod and a Blackberry in my pocket, and yet there were entire families living with no running water, no sewage system, in hovels dug out of rock.

Dr. Xinhua's patient, a little girl he had operated on just a few months previously, was waiting with her parents and sister outside their home.

Li Chuanhui was five years old. Her hair was pulled into two pigtails, and she had on a bright red coat that matched the roses in her cheeks from the frigid cold weather. Li recognized Dr. Xinhua, immediately running to give him at hug, but for the rest of our visit, the little girl clung to her mother's legs, watching these strange Americans warily.

Li's parents led us inside. Their cave was a single room, the shape of a tunnel, with a dirt floor, the damp walls packed with clay. Newspaper was pasted to the walls to try to hold back the dust. They had just a few pieces of furniture—the Chuanhui family slept together on a large stone bed. Next to the bed was a fire for cooking, which sent hot air under the bed to keep them warm at night. Even so, it was freezing. There was no door, just an open entrance to the elements. For water, the family had to walk two miles to the river up and down a very steep hill. A single light hung from the ceiling, without a light bulb. Mr. Chuanhui explained that although the cave was on the electricity grid, they didn't have the money to pay for the bulb. I remember feeling relieved we had come here in daylight. I couldn't imagine what this place felt like at night.

Everything else this family possessed, they grew or made themselves. They had a plot of land the size of a small backyard where they were expected to grow enough food to live on. They owned three chickens but they didn't eat the eggs, because they had to sell them for money. Life was hard enough for the Chuanhui family without adding a child with a cleft into the equation. But what was extraordinary about these parents was that they had chosen to bring little Li into their lives. Although they had an older biological daughter who was 13 years old, their daughter Li was adopted.

Through our interpreter, Mrs. Chuanhui began to tell us her story.

One winter, about five years before, Mrs. Chuanhui was walking to the river to get water, when she passed a box by the side of the road. She could hear crying. Mrs. Chuanhui looked around her. There was no one else on the path. She kept on walking. This was at 9am.

Around lunchtime, she was on her way home from the river when she passed the box. Again she heard crying. She took a look inside and saw a baby girl with a deformed lip, wrapped in a dirty blanket. She kept walking.

At 5pm, the sun was setting. Mrs. Chuanhui went out to see if the box was still there. By now, it was starting to snow. She already had a six-year old daughter— one too many mouths to feed— but she knew she couldn't leave an infant outside to freeze to death. She picked up the box and took the little girl home. The baby weighed just a few pounds, and Mrs. Chuanhui was sure that the little girl was no more than a day old. When she showed the infant to her husband, he couldn't help himself. He picked up the baby and blew on her hands, trying to put some warmth into them.

The couple decided to keep the little girl with the cleft and raise her as their own. They called her Li.

As little Li got bigger, the problem of her cleft became more pronounced. Her teeth began to grow, protruding from the gaping hold in her top lip that made her look grotesque, monstrous even. Someone told them there was a surgery to fix Li's lip, but the Chuanhuis knew they could never afford the surgery. Paying for medical care was never going to be an option for a poor peasant family like this one.

Then, when Li was four years old, Dr. Xinhua came to the village, looking for children with clefts. He found Li playing outside. He told her parents about the surgery. He explained that if they could come to Jingzhu, they would receive the surgery free of charge. They told him they would come, but they had no money to travel. Dr. Xinhua told them he would come back to get them the following week. Li's operation had taken place a month ago. The previous week, the little girl had started school. Her parents told us proudly that she was going to be the first member of her family to learn to read and write.

As we listened to the story, we kept telling Mr. and Mrs. Chuanhui how generous and compassionate they were, what a good thing they had done, but they shrugged their shoulders, as if taking Li home was the only course of action available to them.

As we began to say our goodbyes, Mr. Chuanhui said he had something he wanted to give us. When he came back, he had a bag of grain in his hand. He held it up to me nodding. He was giving me a gift. I knew this family probably didn't have enough food to last the month. It was an awkward moment, to say the least. I shook my head, smiling, trying to refuse. At this point, our interpreter whispered loudly to me that I needed to accept the gift, that it was the local custom to give guests a gift, and that the family would be insulted if I refused. Mr. Chuanhui bowed and gave me the bag. I bowed back to him and thanked him, even if all I wanted to do was give the bag right back to him.

The bag of grain sat beside me on the journey back to the city. I thought about the Chuanhui family. These people had saved the life of a child. They brought her home and raised her. They taken her into their lives when they had nothing—not even enough to feed themselves—and they had done it for no other reason than it was the right thing to do. I live in a place where I can call 911 if I stumble upon a problem I don't want to deal with myself. If I found an abandoned baby on a street corner in Manhattan, the police and social services would take care of the child, and fifteen minutes later I would continue on with my day. There would be no sacrifice involved. I wouldn't have to take responsibility for bringing up a child. These peasants didn't have that luxury. They had no education, no church, no money to look after little Li, and yet they had acted on the most profound moral impulse—they saved the life of a child. On the journey back to Jingzhou, I thought about these parents and I also thought about the extraordinary man in the driver's seat, Dr. Xinhua. Like the Lius, there was no questioning his values, the moral imperatives that shaped his daily life.

I spend a lot of time at Smile Train giving speeches and presentations, showing pictures of children and talking about how "we change their lives." I tell people about Colorful Cloud and the first time I witnessed a cleft surgery and the transformation these children receive through the programs we help to run. But the reality is that I owe a much greater debt of gratitude to these children and their families than they will ever owe to me. They have changed me beyond recognition. My values, my perspective, my view of the world, everything shifts when you look at the world from the point of view of a family who have nothing, and who give everything. I had gone into the Chuanhui home thinking I was the generous one, that I was helping this poor family who had so little. But the reality was, I had left with a gift. The bag of grain represented all the life-changing experiences I'd gained working at Smile Train, how many people I'd met that I never would have encountered if I'd stayed in my comfortable corner of Manhattan. And it was a reminder that ultimately, charity work is not about giving. It's about getting. It's not selfless; it's selfish. Helping others is the most selfish thing in the world, because you always get much more out of it than you put in. Maybe the Chuanhui family understood this. Maybe this was why they had shrugged when he complimented them on what they had done. Maybe taking in a child made them feel like they were making a difference in that bleak and desolate corner of the world.

When we returned back to New York, we made sure that some extra funds were sent to the Chuanhui family. The next thing we did was to send Dr. Xinhua grant money for a new van with excellent brakes. In the end, it was a self-serving gesture—another selfish gesture—because the last thing we wanted was to lose one of the best surgeons Smile Train ever had in the treacherous, bumpy, icy, hairpin roads of the Shanxi hills.

.... TWELVE ....

How to Make A Donor Smile

Six-year-old Georgie Exarchakis was sitting in the waiting room of his doctor's office in New York when he saw a Smile Train pamphlet lying on a table next to him.

Georgie pointed to the picture of a child with a cleft on the cover and turned to his mom, Sophie.

"What's wrong with this boy?" he asked.

"He has a cleft," said Sophie.

Georgie paused.

"Like I had a cleft?" he asked. "Yes, just like you did when you were born," Sophie replied. "If you didn't have your surgery, this is what you would look like."

Georgie stared at the photograph. He frowned and touched his fingers to his mouth. Georgie's lip had been repaired when he was three months old and since then, he had undergone multiple operations to fix the hole in his palate. This little boy had spent the last six years in and out of hospitals and doctors offices; clefts were a part of this family's day-to-day reality. But it wasn't until that moment in the doctor's waiting room in New York that Sophie realized that Georgie had never actually seen a picture of a child with an unrepaired cleft before.

Georgie couldn't stop staring at the photo.

"Why don't they fix it?" he immediately wanted to know.

"Well, some children in other parts of the world are very poor, and they don't have the money to go for surgery," Sophie explained.

Georgie looked even more confused. It made no sense to a five-year-old that there were children in who had to look like this when there was a surgery to help them.

Immediately, he came up with a solution. "Mom, don't you have your checkbook with you?" he asked his mom. "Can't we pay for these children to have surgeries too?"

"Well, we can try," explained Sophie, "But there are a lot of children. I don't think we're going to be able to pay for everyone."

Sophie took the pamphlet home, where she stuck it to the fridge to remind her to send a check.

Later that same week, Georgie's sister, Maria, was selling chocolate bars to raise money for her school, going door to door in the neighborhood. Georgie had an idea.

"I want to do that too," he told his mom. "But I want to get the money for the surgeries."

Sophie smiled at her son. Georgie had gone through so much with his surgeries, but what his cleft had also given him was an ability for empathy beyond his years.

"Great idea," she said. "Let's do that."

Sophie went to get the Smile Train pamphlet and a Coca Cola cup for collecting money. Then Georgie, his sister and his mom went out into their New Jersey neighborhood to knock on doors. Georgie walked up to every house. He was determined. He showed people the pamphlet. He explained to his neighbors that he had been born with a cleft, but that not everyone was lucky enough to have the same surgeries that he'd been given. People immediately reached for their pocketbooks.

After only an hour Georgie's Coca Cola cup was filled three times over.

Sophie and Georgie went home and counted the money. Georgie had raised

$50. Sophie was impressed.

But Georgie was crestfallen.

"I thought I was going to get $5,000!" he exclaimed, adding, "I need to help a lot of children…"

Sophie explained that $5,000 is a large amount of money and that he probably wasn't going to get that walking around the block. After Georgie went to bed that night, Sophie and her husband Jimmy decided they were going to find some way to raise the additional funds. The family worked with their local church youth group to plan a dinner dance that went on to raise $25,000 for the Smile Train. They've raised another $30,000 for us since then from their annual dances, in total enough to pay for around 216 surgeries. As Georgie likes to say, "I put a lot of smiles into the world." This family knew exactly what it means to have a child born with this defect. They knew from first hand experience how challenging it is to feed your baby in the beginning, how difficult it is leaving the house with everyone looking at him and wondering what's wrong, how complicated and stressful it is to go through surgery with a small child. They have never forgotten the day Georgie came home from preschool, went to the bathroom, and covered his lip in Band Aids. "No more boo-boos, no more questions," he said to his mom. Yet Sophie and Jimmy had every advantage available to parents in America: they had expert medical advice, web sites, chat groups, support groups, the support of family and friends. They could only imagine how a parent living in poverty would manage.

Georgie and his parents didn't have to make an imaginative leap in order to reach out and help other children with this problem. They understood completely. But families like Georgie's are amongst the small minority of people in this country. In the U.S., only one in every 700 children is born with a cleft, and all of these babies have their defects repaired. So unless you spend a lot of time traveling in developing countries or unless someone in your family was born with the defect, it's unlikely that you'll ever see an unrepaired cleft, let alone think about what it's like to live with one. Thanks to the huge advances in the availability and quality of cleft surgery in this country, our most common birth defect has become invisible. We don't see clefts and we don't hear about them, precisely because we've made them go away. Even Georgie had never seen an unrepaired cleft until he happened to notice the pamphlet in the waiting room.

This invisibility has been an enormous challenge for Smile Train as we try to mobilize donors and draw them to this cause. People donate to cancer research because they have had experience with family members or friends with cancer. People donate to the homeless and volunteer at soup kitchens because they walk past people on living the streets in our own cities. They give money for disaster relief because they see the images on TV and in newspapers. How do you bring attention to a problem that's not on everyone's radar?

In many ways, it's a conundrum that every charity faces trying to raise money for overseas causes. We live in a world where there are untold numbers of horrifying atrocities happening on the other side of the world that never make the nightly news here in the U.S., that continue to happen out of eyesight. To give one example: every day, 27,000 children under the age of five in developing countries will die from preventable causes. This should be a banner headlines in every newspaper every day of the year, yet it's not, and so it's easy to push a statistic like this to the back of the mind. The numbers are so big, the problem is so vast, that even when we hear this statement, it's too much for the brain to process. The philosopher Peter Singer—who writes about ethics—describes it this way: If you're walking down the street and you see a child drowning in a pond, you don't hesitate, you rush right in to save the child. But when someone tells you that 27,000 children under the age of five will die today, you don't have the same reaction. You feel powerless. You shrug your shoulders and say, "There's nothing I can do about that." People call this the "futility free pass." You can't fix everyone, so you don't help anyone.

It's extremely difficult not to feel overwhelmed by the world's problems. I think the reason that many people in the U.S. prefer to help out within their own communities is because it's much more straightforward. It's more tangible. When I was running my schools program, I could see the kids on the subway that needed surgery with my own eyes. I could get them to come to my office and I could shake their little hands. I felt like I was doing something meaningful because the results were happening right in front of me. Someone who rushes into the pond to save the drowning child is almost certainly going to feel like they achieved something that day. It's much harder to make a leap of imagination and help save someone in another country, because even if you do make that leap, you know you're not going to be able to see the results with your own eyes.

I understand this psychology very, very well, because to be honest, until I started traveling overseas, that's the way I felt too. I knew that people were struggling in other parts of the world, but as far as I was concerned, it wasn't my problem. In fact, back when I was running the schools program, I was a walking poster child for the "charity begins at home" slogan. I remember how much it bugged me every time I went to visit one of my plastic surgeon clients, and his walls would be covered with pictures of him smiling and holding up a kid he'd helped in Africa, China, or India. I would think to myself: "Wow, this doctor flies to Kenya so he can put the photo in his waiting room and impress all his rich clients. And meanwhile, he won't help out a child in his own backyard?" What about American kids? Wasn't the photo-op good enough for him? It made no sense to me that someone would travel thousands of miles to help someone when there were poor kids right here in the United States who needed surgeries. I remember saying at the time, "You know, before you go around the world, you should really go around the block."

I didn't know any better. I had no idea that 99% of the world's suffering takes place outside of America. Like the majority of Americans, I wasn't widely traveled. My idea of an adventure was going to a five star hotel in the Bahamas, or jetting off for a weekend in Paris. And I assumed—wrongly—that there was already far too much U.S. money and energy getting donated to foreign causes. If I was going to help kids, I wanted them to be American kids. I didn't visit a developing country until I was 32, but when I did venture beyond my comfort zone, it changed my life. For the first time I had direct experience of the dire conditions in which over a billion people on this planet spends their lives, where families live on one meal a day if they're lucky because they can't afford breakfast or dinner, where people survive without basic access to drinking water, or electricity, or sanitation, and where poverty breeds disease and misery on such a scale that even the average person living in the West would find so unimaginable, that if they saw such suffering first hand, they would immediately want to do something about it. Those trips didn't only open my eyes; they opened my heart. I knew I wanted to do my part, that I didn't want to turn away.

Sadly, I could wallpaper every bit of our offices with rejection letters from foundations and corporations saying, "I'm sorry, we only help children in Kentucky, or children who live near our stores, or whose families are our customers." Americans give more money every year than any other nation on earth—$229 billion in 2009—but for better or worse, less than 5% goes to help people in developing countries. We are the richest nation on earth, and yet 96% of the money we raise in this country stays within our borders. Imagine if Beverly Hills had a fundraiser that raised millions of dollars for children and said that 96% of it was going to children living in zip code 90210. There would be uproar. But that's what we do in America every year. We give away a massive amount of money, but we give the vast majority of it to ourselves. Of all the challenges we face running Smile Train, fundraising continues to one of our biggest mountains to climb. We have an invisible problem, and not only that, it's happening thousands of miles away. How do we bring this problem home?

Smile Train was extremely fortunate in that for the first two years, we did not need to raise a single nickel. We had enough startup money from Charles Wang and a matching amount from Charles' mentor, Walter Haefner, to be able to focus on building our programs from the ground up. It was a real luxury. But when I took over as President in 2001, we tripled the number of surgeries that first year. This was great news. The bad news was that our soaring program expenses quickly drained our start-up reserves. After a year of running Smile Train, I had to go to our board with a very sobering forecast: at the current rate of program spending we would run out of money in three years. Although Charles would always cover our overhead costs, we had to develop a fundraising capability to pay for our programs, and we had to do it quickly. We were working so hard to make doctors self-sufficient, and yet we had failed to do the same for ourselves.

Our fundraising efforts began the only way I knew how: through advertising. A good friend was able to get us newspaper ads at significant discounts, so we started there. Our first ad was a simple headline that read: Give a child with a cleft a second chance at life.

Below the headlines was a "before" photo of a child with a cleft and an "after" photo of a child post-surgery.

I didn't want the ad to be any more complex than that: clefts are such a visual problem that in this instance, two pictures could truly speak a thousand words. Along with the ad was a coupon with information about how to donate. The response was overwhelmingly positive. As far as I know, we're the only major charity in America that continues to raise significant amounts of money through coupons in newspapers and magazines. When I tell people I work at Smile Train, they will usually respond: "oh, the charity with all the ads in the newspaper." What we've discovered is that by advertising in newspapers, magazines, and online, we can reach people in a way we could never reach them through direct mail. Every week of every year, people get a rainforest's worth of direct mailings from charities in their mailboxes, and most of these envelopes end up in the recycling bin before they're even opened. We do use direct mailings, but we find they are much less effective than our ads, which people see as part of their daily lives. Over the years, we've often had complaints from donors about all the "expensive" Smile Train ads we run and we always explain that all our ads are bought at a substantial discount through negotiation, and that they've helped us bring attention to what is, in effect, an invisible cause. For a long time, all our ads looked the same way: a simple headline and photos of a child "before" and "after" surgery. Then we did some market research and discovered that in fact, people were much more likely to donate if we removed the "after" photo. We were shocked to learn this. We wanted donors to see the amazing transformation that happens to children after they have their clefts repaired! But when we analyzed the responses, we learned that on some subliminal level, the people who'd seen a photo of a child after receiving the surgery felt that the problem had been addressed, that the job was done. This person didn't feel the same urgency to get involved and to donate. But when someone was faced with a photo of a child before surgery, as hard as it was to look at an unrepaired cleft, this person were haunted by it, the same way I was haunted by Soccer Boy, running behind me, when we left that village in Vietnam. That day, I had a sense that something needed to be done and that I had to act. An image like is terrible, but it's motivating. When we started running ads with a single "before" photo of a child, we saw an immediate spike in donations. These are the ads you'll see in newspapers and magazines to this day.

One day, I was reading e-mails from donors, when I came across a brilliant suggestion that gave a purpose to all the miraculous "after" photos in our archives.

"Why don't you send us a photo of a child after surgery so we can see how our money is being spent?" this donor asked.

We loved this idea. Now, when someone donates to us, in addition to a thank you note, we also send a photo of a child "after" surgery. We call these "fridge photos" because our donors pin these postcards to their refrigerators, as a reminder of exactly how they've helped. As a donor myself, I know I'm much happier giving money to charities that can be specific about what they do. A fridge photo is a very simple, inexpensive way to show donors the impact of their generosity. All of us want to feel good about the money we donate, and the fridge photo is just one way of reminding donors that they are making a difference.

Every week I read and answer hundreds of e-mails from donors. When I'm not traveling, I make sure I go regularly into our development department so I can sit and open envelopes. I don't have to do this. I have a staff that can easily send back a "personal response." I could save a lot of time by doing this, but I would miss out on a lot of good feedback, valid complaints, and painful criticisms that help me to be a lot better at my job. I read the notes that come with donations: children's pictures with hand printed scrawls saying "This is $4 from my piggy bank" or "this is $50 that I saved in birthday and Christmas money." Recently I received an e-mail that said: "I just got laid off from my job but I am going to continue to send $25 a month for as long as I can." I try and call to make personal connections with donors whenever I can because the way I see it, donors are our shareholders, and we have a responsibility to make them feel that their money is being well spent. In our early years, we used to receive an annual check for several thousand dollars. When I called the donor up to say thank you, I learned that the man who had given us this money was a widower in his 90s. He lived alone. We struck up a friendship over the phone, and I would call to update him on how his money was being spent. After he passed away, social workers found garbage bags stuffed full of money inside his home. It was all cash intended to be given away to various charities. He left a substantial donation to Smile Train in his will, reminding us that we are the custodians of a tremendous amount of trust and goodwill—and that this is a huge responsibility.

Of course, we're always happy to receive such generous donations, but we're also extremely proud that 95% of our donations are in amounts less than $100, and that our average donation amount is $55. These are the funds that drive our work, that keep Smile Train on the tracks. Americans are the most generous people on earth and although most of the money donated in the U.S. stays in this county, I've always believed if we can find new and innovative ways of making people aware of what's going on in other parts of the world—if we can show them how cheap and effective it is to help a child in need—Americans are going to respond. And they have. We will need to raise many millions before the job is finished and we have helped every child with a cleft that needs us. But with the help of people like Georgie and his family and thousands of other donors all across this country, someday, we will get there.

.... THIRTEEN ....

Christmas in Baghdad

In the spring of 2005, an e-mail arrived in the Smile Train inbox. It was from an army sergeant named Brendan Stephens, stationed in Nasiriyah in Southern Iraq. Each day, the sergeant wrote, Iraqi parents came to his checkpoint, bringing with them children who were sick or injured, begging for his help. The official policy was "life, sight or limb"—if the child was about to lose one of these, then Sergeant Stephens could admit the family to the airbase hospital. Growing up in the U.S., Brendan Stephens had never seen an unrepaired cleft before, and so he was shocked to see so many children with this defect being brought to the checkpoint. Reluctantly, Sergeant Stephens had to tell these parents there was nothing he could do, that other cases had to take priority. The parents pleaded with him to help them, and so the sergeant searched for cleft charities online and found us.

In his e-mail, he asked if we would be willing to help children in Iraq. "Of course," we replied, without hesitation.

At this point in time, however, we didn't have any doctors on the ground in Nasiriyah. Meanwhile, the situation throughout Iraq was highly volatile. It wasn't an option to ask our local doctors in Baghdad to make the treacherous journey south, traveling on roads littered with IEDs. But if we could find an outside team to stage a mission at the airbase, which had its own landing strip and hospital, then the group would be able to fly in and out without endangering anyone.

We started putting wheels in motion. We found an amazing surgeon in the UK who was willing to go to Nasiriyah and he began to put together a team.

Various members of our board were outraged when they heard this news. "You're staging a mission!" "How can you do this?" "Our goal is to empower local doctors." "This is contrary to all our principles!" There were some extremely heated arguments. I remember taking a last minute red-eye back from the West Coast to attend a medical advisory board meeting in New York on a Sunday just to defend this decision. I explained to the board that when we started Smile Train, we were convinced that our "teach a man to fish" model was the new delivery system. We had partner surgeons in hospitals in 60 places in the world, everywhere from Afghanistan to Georgia and Vietnam to Brazil. These numbers only deepened our conviction that the model was working. We were empowering local doctors to substantially increase their numbers of surgeries, measurably improving the quality and safety of the care being provided, and upgrading facilities, not just for cleft patients, but also for every surgical patient at that hospital.

But even so, there were patients in parts of the world that right now, we simply couldn't reach unless we sent a mission.

"This sergeant is telling us that there are cleft patients in Nasiriyah and he is turning them away," I said. "If we can do something about that, we should."

If you'd told me when we started Smile Train that I'd be arguing with our board about the necessity of funding a mission, I never would have believed you. For so long now, I had been virulently against parachuting in Western doctors because I felt they were pushing local doctors aside who were more than capable of doing the work for their own communities. But the more we expanded our reach, the more we realized that there is a place for missions where there's a dire shortage of local surgeons on the ground. I felt we could be stubborn, dig our heels in and wait for the conflict to end in Iraq, or we could act right now.

It had taken visiting our partners in so many countries now, seeing the challenges they face, to finally acknowledge that an organization working on global scale has to continually adapt to conditions on the ground. Our model was absolutely the right way to go in 90% of the developing world, but in places where we couldn't work with local surgeons, missions had their place. I explained to our Board of Directors that "teach a man to fish" was our model, but it wasn't our goal. Our goal is to help children. If we learned that spraying folic acid on wheat fields could reduce the incidence of clefts amongst children in the developing world—and as far as we know, it doesn't—we would spray folic acid on every wheat field we could find. Whatever is the smartest, cheapest best way to help these children, we're going to do it.

In the end, the firestorm over the decision to fund this mission was short lived. We ran into a bureaucratic glitch on the army's side—so the mission was put on hold.

But even so, a philosophical shift had been made. It wasn't just war zones like Southern Baghdad where we lacked surgeons on the ground. In Bangladesh, there are twelve plastic surgeons serving a population of 164 million. Twelve plastic surgeons dealing with emergency burns and trauma victims can't be expected to tackle a backlog of thousands of cleft patients: in fact, it would be unethical to divert them away from the more important work of saving lives. In Kenya there are five plastic surgeons for 35 million people, to give another example. Few medical schools in countries this drastically poor provide training for specialist surgeons, because doing so is too costly and too time-consuming. Again, we could be stubborn and wait another thirty or forty years for the economic situation to improve, and for the medical infrastructure to evolve, or we could offer to fund outside groups who are willing to go into areas to help with the shortfall.

Later that year, we wrote to every overseas mission group doing cleft work that we could find—and we found about 900 of them—inviting them to submit proposals for funding. One of these came from an extraordinary Italian surgeon named Dr. Fabio Abenavoli based in Rome, Italy. In 2007, Fabio launched Smile Train Italy, a group of dedicated medical professionals who will fly in and out of areas where help is desperately needed. In his first two years of operation, Fabio staged missions for Smile Train to Afghanistan, Mozambique, Pakistan, Tanzania, Uganda, and Armenia. Thankfully, very few countries in the world are in such desperate straits that they require a high volume of visits from outside groups like this one. Today, less than 3% of our surgeries are done through overseas mission groups and we envisage that number decreasing as medical provision in the countries where we work increases. But try telling the 4,000 children who are operated on every year in this way that their surgeries aren't important. Every surgery is important, because every surgery helps change a life.

It was Fabio who finally led our mission to Iraq in 2008, flying into Camp Mittica, in Nassyriah, alongside 18 volunteer plastic surgeons, anesthetists, pediatric intensive-care physicians, nurses and logistic experts, bringing with them amazing mobile operating theater donated by the Italian government. Over a period of two days, Fabio and his team operated on 66 Iraqi children and their families. Afterwards, Fabio wrote to us telling us about the mother of a little 7-month-old girl named Duha, from Nasiriyah, was so visibly shaken and overjoyed after seeing her daughter post-surgery, she hugged him and thanked him. With tears in her eyes, she told him, "I believe there is a heaven, and I will gladly give you my place in heaven to thank you for what you have done for my daughter."

The Smile Train Italy mission had been a success, but that didn't lessen our commitment to support our partners in the field. It's estimated that around 1,000 new babies are born with the defect each year in Iraq. Meanwhile, the backlog of existing clefts stands in the region of 20,000. To date, we have four Iraqi cleft surgeons working in Baghdad and its surrounding area and so when we received another e-mail from a soldier in Iraq, Lt. Charles Duggan, stationed in the capital, we could quickly direct him to one of them.

It was late November 2009 when Duggan's his patrol duties had brought him to Abu T'Shir in the Rashid district of southern Baghdad, home to one of the many shantytowns in this area, a part of the city he had never visited before. Ahead of him was what looked like a shallow trash dump, an area the size of a football field, strewn with rubbish, a toxic mix of dust and rubble, broken bottles, plastic bags and twisted, burned-out metal. As his eyes adjusted to the midday sun, Duggan realized that he could make out figures on the dump. A group of children were playing, kicking around a deflated ball. A stray goat ate its way through a bag of rotting scraps. All around the dump perimeter were small makeshift mud huts. Duggan was twenty-three years old, from Jacksonville, North Carolina. He was from a military family and when he signed up for the National Guard, had been more than ready for active duty. Even so, nothing could have prepared him for the sight of those barefoot children playing in the trash outside their homes made of mud.

Duggan sucked in his breath and signaled to the rest of his platoon—the nineteen men of the 252nd Combined Arms Battalion, 30th Heavy Brigade Combat Team—to spread out and to go ahead of him in order to assess the area. The platoon members began handing out candies to the children who inevitably gathered around them. Duggan spotted one boy in the crowd who immediately stood out.

The boy's lip looked like someone had taken a fishhook and yanked the flesh from the top of his mouth right up to his nose. During his time in Iraq, Duggan had seen any number of children who had been injured and maimed due to the conflicts—kids with missing limbs, those who were disfigured by burns or shrapnel—but it was obvious to him that this disfigurement was a birth defect. Even though Duggan had never seen an unrepaired cleft before, a friend his from high school had a scar on his upper lip from the same exact problem and the surgery to fix it. The soldier smiled at the little boy and the boy shyly smiled back. Duggan crouched down to say hello, then pulled a candy out of his pocket and handed it over. The boy grabbed the candy, shoved it in a pocket, then kissed Duggan on the cheek.

"Where's this boy's father?" Duggan asked.

A man with closely cropped hair and large dark eyes, stepped forward. He introduced himself. His name was Rehim.

"How old is the boy?" Duggan asked.

"Three years old," the father replied. "Why hasn't his lip been fixed?"

"We have no money for the surgery," the man said, looking around him at the desolation, as if by way of explanation.

The interpreter explained that the man was called Rehim and that his son was Abdulla. The father showed the soldier how the hole in Abdulla's lip extended into the roof of his mouth right up to his nose cavity. Abdulla had trouble eating, speaking, and hearing. Food would get trapped in his nose. Fluid from his nose would become blocked in his ears.

"Life is very, very hard for him," the father said, shaking his head.

Rehim told Duggan their story. Abdulla was born at the Al Qadra Hospital in Baghdad in 2007. Since they brought the baby home, the family sufferings had only increased. When they left the house, people would turn away from them. The villagers told Rehim and Hamida that no man would consider marrying into a family with a child like Abdulla They told the parents that because of his lip and mouth, Abdulla would be mentally impaired. Rehim had two daughters. He contemplated what he was going do with two unmarried girls and a son who couldn't go to school or leave the house. This man was a laborer, making daily wages, barely enough to feed and clothe his family. Every night, he would stay awake late into the night, thinking about Abdulla, and what could be done.

Abdulla's throat was continually and painfully inflamed because of the hole in the roof of his mouth. He had chest infections. His little body was made of skin and bone because he could never eat enough. Even by the standards of the other children of Abu T'Shir, he was malnourished. By the age of three, he was making attempts to communicate, but his missing palate made it impossible for him to produce words—instead, what came out of his mouth were garbled sounds that even his parents struggled to interpret. Abdullah spent most of the day at home. He didn't like being around people or other children. The day he stepped out to see the American soldiers had been the exception: he'd wanted to have some candy, just like all the other children, even if it was impossible for him to eat it.

Duggan thought about what it must be like for any of these children, living in a war zone, in a shantytown in one of the most dangerous places on earth—let alone a child with a defect. When he left that day he promised Rehim that he would try to do something to help.

Two weeks after his first visit, Duggan returned to Abu T'shir. It was the 23rd of December, right before Christmas, which happened to coincide that year with the Muslim festival of Hajj. Duggan's platoon had brought muffins and soft drinks as a Hajj gift for the children who flocked around the men the moment they arrived.

When Duggan found Rehim, he told him that he had brought Abdulla a gift for Hajj as well. He handed Rehim a slip of paper. As Rehim read it, his eyes filled with tears.

Written in Arabic on the paper was the address and contact information for Dr. Ahmed Nawres, at Hilla General Teaching Hospital in Babylon, south of Baghdad, and the following words: "This doctor will operate on Abdulla free of charge."

"There are no words in any language to express how I feel right now," Rehim told the soldier.

For his part, Duggan was only thankful that he had been able to do something to help because he didn't think he could live with himself otherwise.

A week after Duggan delivered the note, Abdulla's surgery was scheduled. The operation was a success— his lip and the floor of his nose were closed. Later that week, Duggan came to see Abdulla. The little boy ran to hug the soldier. There was a large Band-aid across his upper lip hiding his stitches, but even so, the transformation was complete.

"Now he opens the door and plays with everyone," Rehim said. "He is three years old, but even at such a young age, he can knows that something is different now." For Abdulla's parents, a weight had been lifted from their shoulders.

Three months after Abdulla's first surgery, the little boy needed a second surgery to close his palate. Again the surgery was a success. By now, Duggan's tour of duty had ended and he had returned to the United States. Somehow, Rehim managed to find a friend of a friend with an e-mail address who could help him send Duggan an e-mail. In broken English, it said, THANK YOU.

Abdullah's family had been waiting for three years for surgery, and yet within three weeks of Duggan e-mailing the Smile Train offices, Abdulla had his first opera tion. Even in a city in the midst of violent conflict, dedicated doctors like Dr. Nawres continue to operate, despite the risk, and in areas that are extremely dangerous for foreign doctors and health workers. The sooner we can reach children, especially those with cleft palates, the greater the opportunity that they will grow up without further health problems or speech impediments. After the age of three, it becomes extremely difficult to change a child's speech habits. Fortunately for Abdulla, Duggan found him right around his third birthday. And thanks to Dr. Nawres—who manages to operate on twelve children like Abdulla every month—this little boy will be able to talk, to play and go to school, without his deformity standing in his way.

"If I can improve this one child's situation," Duggan told us in his e-mail. "I will feel as though I am succeeding at what I came here to do." Every time those parents looked at Abdulla—every time anyone living in Abu T'shir looked at Abdulla—they were reminded of an American soldier and his act of kindness. Lt. Duggan had gone into Abu T'shir handing out candies, hoping to win hearts and minds, but he had left behind something more powerful—he had helped to right a wrong. Whether it's the rare occasion we have to stage a mission in a war zone or whether we can have local surgeons do the work, that's always going to be the goal.

.... FOURTEEN ....

Tracking Smiles

In 2008, Smile Train hosted a small thank you dinner in London for a group of our donors from the UK. Special guests that night included member of parliament called Shailesh Vara, a rising star in British politics who gave a very impressive speech about the importance of giving back to society. I stood up and did my usual slide show. But the person who stole the show that night was a man called Henry Foster.

Foster was an elderly man, smartly dressed in a three-piece suit, leaning on an elegant wooden cane. The moment you saw him, you could tell that something was wrong. In fact, your eyes couldn't avoid it—his upper lip on the right side was badly mangled.

By now, I knew enough about clefts to guess that Foster had been born with a cleft, that it had been repaired, but that the repair was a bad one.

"I am told there are 24 people attending this dinner," Foster began. "I can tell you with some certainty that 23 of you share one thing in common with each other, but not with me. None of you have clefts."

When Foster spoke, his voice was nasal, and it was hard for him to enunciate. I'm sure many people assumed he was deaf or hard of hearing. By now, I knew that this in all likelihood he'd received cleft palate surgery, but that it had somehow gone awry.

I guessed correctly. Henry Foster explained that he had been born in London in 1924 with a severe cleft lip and palate. In the first week of his life, his parents were unable to find a special bottle so that they could feed him. As a result, Foster's weight dropped so dangerously low, that he nearly died.

"My cleft was a terrible shock for my parents," Foster remembered. "An unimaginable horror for them. They asked themselves over and over again, what had they done to deserve this. But somehow I survived, because I am now 83 years of age."

Before Foster's first birthday, his parents managed to find a surgeon for him, and his defect was repaired. But in 1924, techniques for repairing clefts were still at an extremely rudimentary stage. Cleft surgeries have existed in some form or another since the beginning human history—the Chinese have records of lip repairs dating back to 390 B.C.—but it was only with the development of anaesthesia in the late 19th century and early 20th century that surgeons could begin to develop their techniques with any degree of sophistication. Modern reconstructive plastic surgery was born in the UK in during World War 1 when a surgeon called Dr. Harold Gillies began operating on soldiers who had suffered traumatic injuries. But children with clefts would have to wait until the late 1950s for innovations in cleft surgery that allowed their lips to be restored to an approximation of natural appearance.

It didn't help that Foster's cleft lip and cleft palate was so severe that he needed to have multiple surgeries. He remembered his weeks spent in hospitals waiting for and recovering from his operations, during which time he developed a terror of men wearing white coats.

"I would scream when anyone with a white coat came near me," he recalled, "to the point where my surgeon learned to take off his coat before coming into the room." When the surgeries were over, Foster still had a highly visible scar on his upper lip, and because of his cleft palate his speech was badly affected. At school, the other children bullied him because of his strange voice and his twisted mouth. At one point his mother even advised him to hit back at his tormentors.

"I never did," Foster recalled sadly. "Does any bullied child?"

After he finished school, Foster was conscripted into the army. It was only after his return to civilian life at the age of 23 that he received an additional surgery to correct his scar.

"But in many ways, the surgery had come to late," he told us. "The physical scar from my cleft was improved, but the memory of everything I had endured remained."

As Foster delivered his speech, I was aware of the young couple at my table who had just given birth to a baby with a cleft lip. They both had tears in their eyes. They looked terrified. I wanted to reassure them that their child would never have to suffer in the way that Foster had suffered. In modern times, techniques for repairing clefts have improved and developed beyond recognition. Today, you can look at a child who has undergone a good cleft lip surgery and barely notice a scar. High quality surgery and follow up care means that children with cleft palates can learn to speak as if their defect had never existed. Modern surgery, done well, can restore a child to normal function, on every level—physically, emotionally, and psychologically—so that children who receive first-rate care go on to forget that their clefts ever existed.

Forgetting wasn't an option for Henry Foster.

"My cleft became burned into my brain," he described. "I am 83 years old, but there isn't a day that passes when I don't think about my defect. It may be a person walking by, a voice I hear, a face I notice, or a Smile Train advertisement I see in the daily newspaper. It doesn't take much to trigger that half-second flashback reminder. My cleft was repaired all those years ago, but it has never gone away. To all you volunteers working for the Smile Train organization in any of the 90 countries of the world where your skill and dedication transforms the lives of so many children for their lifetime: I applaud and appreciate the work you carry out with such zeal and enthusiasm.

To those of you giving donations, I thank each of you for your generosity. Just £150 enables every child to have a life changing operation that enables each one to rejoin its community and their peers, and enables them to get an education that is of enormous benefit to each patient and the community within which he or she thrives.

Foster is a powerful example of what happens to someone who receives an inadequate surgery and a reminder that cleft surgery isn't inherently good. Bad surgeries can create their own problems. Our partner surgeons regularly see older patients whose lips and palates have been wrecked by a prior, less competent doctor, and who have to undergo further surgeries to correct the damage. As an organization, Smile Train can provide the necessary funding for a surgery, but if that surgery leaves a terrible scar—if the child has to go back for more surgeries to correct a prior surgery—that child may be just as traumatized as if his cleft was never repaired at all. The goal of a cleft surgery isn't just to plug a hole; it's to rehabilitate children and restore them to normal appearance and function so that they can go on with their lives, as their clefts never existed. If we fail to deliver quality surgeries, children will continue to suffer, even after their clefts have been repaired.

In 2008, Smile Train virtual surgery DVD finally launched—directly inspired by the need to find new and innovative ways of improving the quality of surgeries amongst our partners. Seven years after Dr. Cutting began developing the project, it was complete. The DVD included 3-D demonstrations of every cleft surgery technique, innovation, and improvement of the past thirty years. Court had consulted with the major experts in the field, creating an encyclopedia of modern cleft surgery: dozens of detailed animations that a surgeon could use to improve, refine, and stimulate his thinking and his skills. In textbook form, so much information would be contained in multiple volumes. As a DVD it fit on two discs that cost 7 cents to copy and could be shipped anywhere in the world.

When we began working on the DVD project, we were excited about its potential, but I don't think any of us realized the degree to which that potential would be realized and even surpassed. We had thought that the animations would be a nice supplement to reading about surgeries in a book or observing actual surgeries in an operating room. Instead, the animations went far beyond 2-dimensions and even beyond reality itself. As a medium for communication, our surgeons told us, the animations are immediate and clear. Each animation shows the anatomical strata of the face—the skin, the fat, the muscle, the cartilage, the bone—in brightly colored, highly visible layers. In an operating room, these layers are obscured by blood making it difficult to see exactly how the surgical technique is being executed. But 3-D animations effectively allow the viewer to see though blood, so that it becomes immediately obvious exactly how each flap of flesh is made and realigned. The animations can also give perspective on areas that simply aren't visible in reality, some of them deep in the mouth and nose. This DVD that was created for surgeons in developing countries is now considered so effective that it's already become a standard training tool for surgeons in the U.S. and Europe, and in every major medical university and teaching hospital in the world. To date, we've shipped more than 75,000 of these DVDs all over the globe.

Since the DVD was launched in 2008, Court and his collaborator Aaron Oliker continue break new ground in the realm of surgical training. As I write this, they are working on an interactive cleft surgery simulation program for Smile Train—the first of its kind. This surgical "video game" will allow surgeons, medical residents, and students to practice cleft surgeries on a computer in 3-dimensions and in real time. It's hard to believe, but while airline pilots have been practicing their skills on flight simulators, surgeons have been practicing their skills on actual people. When this software is complete, however, medical students will be able to try out surgical techniques on the computer, before they ever operate on another human being. They will be able to practice until they've reached a good skill level, making cuts in virtual skin, pulling back flaps to reveal virtual tissue layers, and examining these layers from different perspectives. The "cleft game" will be able to test each student, make suggestions, ask questions, and give grades. When it is finished, we believe it will revolutionize the way cleft surgery is taught all over the world.

From the beginning, we had said that technology was going to be the ace up our sleeve. Twelves years later, it's enabled us to scale up and help hundreds of thousands of children, while maintaining a tiny staff of 44. Our ability to track and monitor surgeries thanks to our digital patient database has been one of the reasons we've stayed streamlined. From the beginning, we were aware that tracking safety and quality was going to present a huge challenge for us. Patient safety needed to be our number one priority, but on the other hand, we couldn't continually visit doctors all over the world to check up on their results—the costs and logistics of such an endeavor would be enormous. Meanwhile, we were asking surgeons working thousands of miles away to do surgeries on our behalf, and in countries where corruption and fraud is all too common. To a large extent, we've circumvented the problem of a hospital defrauding us because we vet our partners extremely carefully—we deliberately select hospitals that already have programs in place to help poor patients, who have been helping their communities for years, so it's highly unlikely that they were going to be interested solely in increasing revenue. But even so, we couldn't just throw money out into the world without a thoughtful system of checks and balances.

Back when I first came on board as president, we began developing a digital patient database that would enable us to log and assess every surgery. The price tag for going digital was high—and many people balked—but I had done enough database advertising for Charles Wang's Computer Associates to know that going digital would save us thousands of dollars in the long run.

There was no doubt that making the switch from paper to digital was a major undertaking. We were working with partners in remote parts of the world with little or no existing high-tech equipment. We had doctors who didn't even own a manual typewriter, let alone a computer. The software for the database included an online application and an off-line application for the hospitals that were going to be accessing the Internet through slow dial-up modems. We bought our partner hospitals new computers and printers, digital cameras. We persuaded and begged until all our partners agreed to switch from paper charts to submitting digital patient charts to us via the Internet. With the software in place, we could access the patient database at any time and see exactly how many surgeries took place on any given day, and which partner hospitals completed them. We could view "before" and "after" photos of every patient operated on by any doctor in the program. The side benefit of going digital was that our doctors began keeping excellent records, which is, after all, good medical practice.

Our goal was to help many thousands of children every month. As a small team, we could never have possibly managed that type of volume the old-fashioned way, with hard copies being stored and shipped half way around the world. But with a database in place, for every patient chart that came into our server, the transaction costs were zero. When we started work on a digital patient database, we knew it was going to be a good cost-saving measure. We hadn't realized that it was going to evolve into something even more important—a high effective means of monitoring and grading doctors for quality and safety. Once the database was in place, we hired Dr. Eric Hubli, a talented pediatric cleft and cranial facial surgeon out of Texas to scrutinize a random sampling of cases from the database each month and to give us his assessment of the work. Dr. Hubli is one of the best and brightest of a new generation of cleft surgeons in this country. Together with the medical advisory board, he came up with a system of grading surgeries based on our digital charts. He looked at the "before" surgery and "after" surgery photographs, and the information in the charts. He came up with a "before" rating (based on the severity of the cleft) and an "after" (based on the success of the operation). By multiplying both these numbers by each other, he came up with a number between one and 25, with one being the lowest score for a simple cleft, and 25 being a perfect score for a very difficult cleft.

As we began to amass a larger and larger number of scored doctors, we realized that Hubli's careful assessments were giving us a very reliable quality rating system. At any given moment, we could name our ten best surgeons and our ten worst surgeons. We could see if a surgeon was succeeding, and we could see if he was failing—if he was using an unsophisticated technique, or if he was operating too quickly or too slowly (the meta data in the patient charts tell us the length of each surgery as the before and after photographs are taken in the operating room). This information has allowed us focus our training on the surgeons who really need our help, rather than wasting time and money on big, general "one size fits all" trainings. Before our grading system was in place, it was hard to design trainings when we couldn't easily know the skill level of the participants. We would gather groups of doctors together for training days and what would inevitably happen afterwards was that various surgeons in the group would tell us they were bored to tears because they had learned nothing new; for others in the group, the information they'd gleaned was vitally helpful. After the database grading system was in place, we could train doctors in groups according to their actual skill level. The grading system also meant we could pinpoint a specific surgeon and fly that doctor to New York to train with members of our medical advisory team if necessary. Other times we would have a doctor from the U.S. visit that surgeon on his home turf. Better still, we could turn the case over to our medical advisory board in the relevant country. We found that sending a local expert to help another doctor improve his skills was a very effective education model: when a doctor receives input from a peer with whom he can easily communicate, his training is more likely to have a meaningful impact. It is an extremely rare case where we need to cut someone from the program altogether. Our policy is always to invest in making doctors better at their work, because if we let someone go, we're aware that doctor will most continue to operate on patients with or without the support of Smile Train.

When we began working on our database, we didn't realize there was anything particularly innovative about this idea. We assumed that the medical industry was applying technology to solve problems just like everyone else. As it turned out, the database was ahead of its time. As I write this, only 5% of all hospitals in the United States have digital patient charts. In 2009, President Obama allocated $20 billion in the new healthcare budget to computerize American hospitals, but we're not there yet. Sadly, patients in the U.S. are a long way from having any kind of quality rating guide for their doctors, because no one is yet systematically collecting medical data and analyzing it. What's more, there's a real resistance in the medical community to this because if you identify your best surgeon, you also have to identify your worst surgeon and no one wants to admit that they have doctors who are at the bottom of the pile. In other words, cleft patients in developing countries have a real advantage over their Western counterparts: they are guaranteed a good surgeon, because if a Smile train doctor has failing scores, we will be able to see that he is failing, his work is flagged, and we can immediately intervene. As we began to extract more and more information from the database, we were amazed by the high standards of care we were seeing. What we discovered was that doctors with poor grades were in a very small minority. We had some extremely talented surgeons in the program, and we watched as they continued to improve with financial support and improved infrastructure. We had founded Smile Train in part because we believed the medical mission model was outdated and patronizing to local doctors, but we soon realized that we had been guilty of condescension ourselves. We had gone into this work suspicious of local doctors and their abilities—we felt they weren't capable of performing surgeries without our training and help. A few years down the line, the database was telling us that surgeons in developing countries were doing exceptional work, and for one very good reason: in countries with large backlog of clefts, a local surgeon has the opportunity to do a much higher volume of cases than his counterpart in the U.S. or Europe. Volume is just as valuable as education and training in this respect because for surgeons, practice makes perfect. While a surgeon in the U.S. is likely to see around fifty cleft cases a year, we have surgeons in China who turn over 500 clefts a year. Ten years ago in the UK, hospitals were asked to reduce the pool of surgeons operating on clefts across the country, because these doctors weren't getting enough time in the operating room to maintain a consistently good standard. Conversely, we see surgeons coming into Smile Train program with mid-level grades who rise quickly to the higher grades as they are given the financial support to do more surgeries and refine their skills through additional training and education. So our model of "teach a man to fish" should more accurately be described as "enable a man to fish more, so that he can learn to fish better."

Many members of our American medical advisory board admitted to me that they are not only impressed by the work of our partner doctors, but frequently humbled by it. Dr. Hubli tells the story of a visit he made to the Guangxi Autonomous Regional Hospital, in one of China's southernmost provinces, where he observed a local surgeon at work. When Dr. Hubli first met this particular surgeon, called Dr. Pan, he thought that he looked very young, and so he was immediately wary, assuming that the Chinese doctor was extremely inexperienced. Hubli then watched in dismay as Dr. Pan made incision after incision in the patient's lip, over 25 cuts in total.

"Thank goodness I'm here and I can help this idiot clear up this mess!" Dr. Hubli remembered thinking to himself.

And then, Dr. Hubli watched in amazement as Dr. Pan sewed the child's lip with a series of tiny and intricate stitches, his fingers moving over the patient's face with exquisite skill. Within five minutes, the repair was finished and it was perfect.

"That's fantastic," Hubli enthused to the doctor after the surgery was complete. "I never saw anyone do it that way before."

Dr. Pan was pleased at the compliment. He disappeared and soon returned with a copy of an article he had written on his technique that had been published in a major Chinese journal ten years ago. This man had been practicing his technique for ten years. Dr. Hubli is one of the most distinguished cleft surgeons in America, but the lip repair he witnessed that day remains one of the best he's ever seen.

"We have so much to learn from everyone," Dr. Hubli told me when he returned from China, "If we're just prepared to open our eyes."

.... FIFTEEN ....

Smile Pinki

In 2009, The Smile Train had a landmark year. We celebrated our tenth anniversary and reached the 500,000 surgery mark. It was also the year we won an Oscar.

The idea behind the project was pretty simple. Movies are the most powerful and popular medium for telling stories in the world right now, so why not make a movie to help us raise awareness about clefts? Not only would the film highlight the problem for people here in the U.S., but we could also use the movie to raise awareness in the countries where we work, where it's an ongoing challenge to educate families about the defect. Just as we had created a DVD to help elevate the knowledge of our doctors, if we could have a DVD that health workers and social workers could show to families to prove to them that clefts can be repaired and that free surgeries are available, then maybe we could elevate the knowledge of our patients too.

In 2007, we commissioned the independent filmmaker Megan Mylan to go to India to film the lives of two children living in rural villages—a girl called Pinki and a boy called Ghutaru—and the journey they take to GS Memorial Hospital in Varanasi. The film follows these children from their homes as they arrive in the big city for the first time, and it shows them when they return home, where they are able to start school. It's an incredibly simple yet moving film that brilliantly captures how these children suffer and how their lives are changed so dramatically by the surgery.

Not only does the film show us the lives of the children, it also shines a light on some unsung heroes of this work: local social workers. When the film begins, we see a social worker called Pankaj Kumar from the GS Memorial Hospital in Varanasi distributing fliers, and putting up posters to help raise awareness for the program in the city. Soon after, we see Pankaj driving out into a tiny village called Rampur Dabai, about an hour outside Varanasi. In the big cities, we can put advertisements in the newspapers and paint notices on walls, but in rural villages like these, Pankaj knows, the best way to reach these patients is to seek them out and meet them face-to-face.

Lack of education continues to be a huge obstacle in this work and in the lives of children we seek to help. For a child with a cleft, the physical defect itself is exactly the problem. That child can live with a cleft. It's not pleasant, but it's possible. Instead, it's the social stigma, the superstition, the assault to a child's confidence, self-esteem, and ability to function in the world that make this defect such a tragedy for these children. It's not just patients and families we need to educate in this respect; it's entire communities. It's medical workers, midwives, nurses and local doctors. Everyone needs to know that this problem is a birth defect and it can be addressed with surgery, and that no child should be shunned and sidelined because of it. Social workers like Pankaj travel many hundreds of miles every month, helping us educate families, their communities, and local health workers who are often just as ill informed as the families.

When he arrives at Rampur Dabai, Pankaj makes straight for the local school.

"A cut lip is nothing to feel shame about," he explains to a classroom of young school children. "The surgery is simple and it is free. Tell the people in your village, they can come to Varanasi for help."

One of the children in the class tells him about a girl in the village called Pinki, and after he finishes speaking to the children, Pankaj goes in search of the family.

He finds Pinki's father, Rajendra Sonka, and her mother, Shimla Devi; outside the small mud hut they share with eight-year-old Pinki and her grandmother.

"She got it because of the eclipse," Pinki's grandmother tells Pankaj, a superstition that this social worker has heard many, many times. He carefully explains to this family that a "cut lip" is called a cleft and that it's a very common birth defect. He tells Pinki's family that if they come to Varanasi on the 18th March, they can have Pinki screened and she'll receive her surgery free of charge.

"The health worker told us we had to have it fixed before her teeth came in," said the grandmother. "It's too late now."

All too often families are misinformed by local health workers—and Pankaj has to convince the family that surgery is possible at any age.

Pankaj can see that he's making progress. Even so, he has to reassure the family that the surgery will be free and that The Smile Train will pay for their travel expenses. "I have barely enough to feed them all," Rajendra explains. "If I had money, it would already be done." Pinki has four brothers and sisters. Her father works in the fields for daily wages. During the harvest and planting seasons, they may have money to buy extra food, but the rest of the year they survive on what they can store or plant themselves. So many of poor families like this one have been told that there's nothing anyone can do, or that they have been cursed by God, that when they hear about free surgery, they have a hard time believing it. Many times, a social workers like Pankaj will have to spend hours explaining, cajoling, and convincing families that a solution really exists.

Even after Pinki's father agrees to come on the 18th, Pankaj has repeatedly reassure him that the operation is going to be free of charge and that the only cost to the family would be money for food.

"Do we have to pay the hospital any money?" Rajendra asks for the third time.

"No, people donate money, it comes to the hospital, and we provide the surgeries," Pankaj repeats again.

"Had I known, I would have got it done when she was born," says Pinki's father, shaking his head. "Now she will be able to lead a decent life and get married one day." Later that same month, our partner surgeon in Varanasi, Dr. Subodh Singh operated on Pinki's cleft, fixing her lip with an operation was completed in less than an hour.

In the film, we see the doctor after he's finished, leaving the operating room to see Pinki's father.

"Everything went fine, absolutely fine," he says. "There is nothing to worry about."

The father puts his hands together and thanks the doctor, bowing his head, on the verge of tears. Pinki has waited nearly nine years for a 45-minute surgery to change her life.

"Have you eaten?" asks Dr. Subodh.

"I will eat after I see my child," says the father. And at this moment every parent watching the film is reminded that when it comes to our kids, no matter where we live in the world, we're all the same.

Smile Pinki is so simple and powerful that as soon as it was shown at film festivals, it began to attract a lot of attention. After it was nominated for an Oscar, though, for a brief period of time, it seemed as if the world went Pinki crazy. In India, hundreds of newspapers and TV news outlets ran stories about Smile Pinki. Pinki and Dr. Subodh went on a five-city tour to screen the film to thousands of people. In the month after we won the Oscar, our partner surgeons in India were inundated with new patients and reported an additional 1,500 surgeries. Soon afterward, we gave Doordarshan, the largest TV network in India, a license in perpetuity to broadcast the film. This state-owned network exists to show educational materials to the masses—it reaches 900 million people in India, many who watch in local meeting halls, home to the only TV in the village. Three or four times a year, Smile Pinki is on TV and every time it runs, our patient numbers in India spike again. Pinki's father, Rajendra, has since gone on national TV and said that he hopes this film shows that having a child with a cleft is not a curse; it is a blessing. Pinki has been to the White House in India several times. The film has also helped us enormously here at home. After it was nominated for an Oscar, it was licensed to HBO, where it was watched by millions of Americans, many of whom became new donors. We sent it to more than a million existing donors who loved it and let us know that it had helped to reaffirm their commitment. (If you would like to see Smile Pinki, you can e-mail me at brian@surgery4thepoor.org and I will send you one.)

I'm happy to report that both children in the film, Pinki and Ghutaru, are well and thriving. Our team in India make sure that they're going to school and that their families are taken care of. After Pinki's Oscar win was announced, a reporter for a local Varanasi newspaper went to Pinki's village to interview her friends and neighbors.

"We are singing and dancing to celebrate this victory," said one villager. "The whole village is celebrating. Pinki, the girl we always used to tease because of her cleft lip, today the whole country is calling her name with pride."

The little girl who had never left her village before she came to Varanasi for surgery—and who had never seen a film until she starred in one, and who had never worn a pair of shoes until she came to Hollywood to walk the red carpet—is now responsible for bringing thousands of cleft children out of their anonymity and bringing just as many new donors to this cause.

But even with Pinki's help, we still struggle with awareness in countries all over the world. The question remains, how do you reach people who live in complete media darkness; who don't have electricity, let alone TV sets; who are by and large illiterate; who don't read newspapers, or listen to the radio? This was a challenge I never faced on Madison Avenue. For the first twelve years of Smile Train's existence, we've been doing outreach the old fashioned way, by sending social workers into the hard-to-access areas, in their cars and vans, on bicycles and motorbikes. But a social worker may have to canvass multiple villages and travel dozens of miles to find even a single child. More recently, we're realizing that we have a huge untapped resource when it comes to spreading the word about clefts and about the availability of surgeries: our patients. The person who alerted us to this idea was Dr. Subodh, the same doctor featured in Smile Pinki.

What Dr. Subodh told us was this: Every time he discharges a patient after surgery, he brings the family to his offices. After the usual pleasantries, he turns to them with a request.

"Now you must pay," he says.

Of course, the poor parents are shocked and their jaws drop, because they don't have any money to pay and they've been told the surgery is free. Then Subodh tells them something else.

"You must pay us for your surgery by going back to your village and finding another child who suffers with a cleft and telling them to come here, to me, for help."

At this point, the patient or the family member is so relieved that they immediately agree to Subodh's terms. Dr. Subodh and his team currently help over 3,500 each year at GS Memorial. This is one of our most prolific hospitals, and part of the reason is that they enlist the help of every single family who comes to the hospital in tracking down more patients. "You are our heroes," Subodh and his colleagues say. "Find us more children with clefts."

What Subodh and our other partners have discovered is that patients and their families are extremely motivated outreach workers. Many of them have been living with the defect for years. They come from hundreds of kilometers just to get to the hospital. They overcome unimaginable obstacles in order to receive this surgery. It's extremely rare to meet a patient or family member who takes this surgery for granted. The vast majority of these families are extremely thankful, and they want to do something in return. They know that they've been given a second chance, and they want others in the same situation to have the same opportunity. When you know how much you've been helped, it's only natural to want to pay it forward.

What we're learning is that our patients are our most powerful agents for communication and education. When a child with a cleft returns to their home after surgery, everyone in the community can see firsthand that it's possible to have this defect fixed, and that it truly can be done for free. In other words, after surgery, our patients become walking advertisements for the program. We've started sending all our patients home with a simple, colorful kids backpack with our logo on it. Inside the backpack is a little brochure containing photos of every conceivable kind of cleft and a short informational blurb in 20 different languages: "This is not a curse from God. Bring your child to a hospital to get it fixed. If you are poor, find a Smile Train hospital. There is one near you because this is where this backpack came from." Then we list all of the locations of these hospitals around the world. In the past two years we've sent home 200,000 of these backpacks that cost us just $3 to make, and our partners tell us they pay enormous dividends. Thousands of children have come to us from this unorthodox referral service.

Some patients have been so successful at bringing in new patients that they are now officially employed by our hospitals as outreach workers, going into outlying areas to help spread the word about the program. Parents of a patient living in a tiny village called Rajnagar in West Bengal have started their own small NGO, organizing registration camps for us. The Mandal had a long and difficult road to finding a doctor to operate on their child, Subhdeep. When his mother went to her local doctor seven days after he was born, the doctor told her that there was nothing he could do for her, that he was too busy to help. A few months later, the family heard about a medical treatment camp taking place in a nearby city, so they traveled there for help. At the treatment camp, these parents were told to go to Kolkata for surgery. Next they went to Kolkata, and visited two hospitals, where they were told that the chances of repairing the boy's lip and palate were not good—he had a bilateral cleft lip and palate— and both doctors they spoke with weren't sure they would be able to fix such a complicated defect successfully.

Then she saw a poster for a Smile Train registration camp taking place 50km away. They decided to make the trip. At the camp, they met our partner surgeon Dr. Tapadar. They told him everything they had been through, the advice they had been given, and that they believed that the boy's defect was going to be difficult to repair. Dr. Tapadar examined the baby.

"Don't worry," he said. "Everything will be all right. Make an appointment for the surgery and have faith." Dr. Tapadar's hospital was 600km away, but his words calmed the family and they made the appointment. In order to get to Varanasi, they had to travel 200km by bus over dirt roads. After a whole day on the bus, they traveled another 400km by train. More than 24 hours after they left their home, they arrived in Varanasi and took a rickshaw to the hospital.

While Subhodeep was still recovering from his surgery, his parents went to Dr.

Tapadar. They thanked him profusely. They also told him they wanted to help others in the same situation.

"Can we organize a camp for you in our area?" they asked. The doctor told them that if they could find a venue and enough volunteers for the camp, and if they could keep good documentation and accounting of expenses, that he was happy to support them. In order to be completely transparent, the family founded and registered a small NGO. Since 2006, their group has helped organize more than thirty outreach camps in their home state of West Bengal, as well as in the neighboring states of Bihar and Jharkhand. They always bring Subhodeep to the camps. They show the child to the families gathered there. They tell them that they traveled over 600km to have Subhodeep's cleft fixed, but that it was worth it, and that the hospital reimbursed them for travel expenses. Instead of having to cajole and even beg doubtful families to come for treatment, these parents can connect directly to other patients, and when people see Subhodeep—with his cleft repaired—they have no option but to believe her. Today, the Mandal family is responsible for encouraging over a thousand patients to leave their villages and to travel many hundreds of kilometers for their surgeries.

The question we have to ask ourselves—the same question we always ask—is how can reach more and more patients? In 2010, we began piloting a new program in six of our partner hospitals. Instead of a backpack, we're giving every patient a SmartPhone, donated by a major phone company. We tell these patients that they can take this phone home with them on one condition: they need to find new patients for us. We also tell them that for every patient they refer to us, we will give them $25 in cash. This is an enormous amount of money for a family making a few dollars a day. Then we show our patients how to use the phone to play a video about the surgery. Once they've convinced the prospective patient, they can call our partner hospital and a trained medical professional does a consultation over the phone, reviews a photo sent via the phone, and schedules an appointment right away. When that new patient comes in for surgery, we pay the bonus to the original patient. In many cases, we can actually use the phone to do this: in some parts of developing countries you no longer need a bank to receive money, you can bring your phone to a special kiosk that reads the information on your phone and gives you your cash.

In the year 2010, cell coverage is already reaching 80% of the world's population (and that figure is growing all the time). People are using mobile phone technology in all kinds of new and innovative ways to significantly improve the lives of the poorest people on the planet—the so-called "bottom billion". Phones are revolutionizing the way farmers plant, harvest, and sell their crops in Africa. There are new applications that teach literacy through mobile phones. The Nobel prize-winner Grameen Bank has given 800,000 phones to "phone ladies" in Bangladesh, who make money from going around their communities selling phone calls to people who have no phones of their own. These new cell users are finding ways to charge their phones using inexpensive car batteries and generators. One of our doctors in Uttar Pradesh, Dr. Khanna, has started working with a local mobile phone company to send out SMS blasts to its users. Within four days of sending out one of these mass messages, more than 1,400 people called the hospital to find out more.

In the coming years, our goal is to use mobile phones to enable us to build an "army" of cleft awareness workers that can cover all of the poor villages and slums that we've had such a hard time reaching through traditional methods. The impact and potential of this human network could go far beyond clefts. Patients could send back information to their hospital on all kinds of other medical conditions. What makes us so confident that this idea will work is the patients themselves. When people watch Smile Pinki and see Pinki after her surgery, they know exactly what it means to have a cleft repaired. When the Mandal family take their son boy to the camps they arrange, no one can doubt that a cleft can be fixed. What we have discovered is that when patients share their stories—when they tell others that they have prevailed, that this is possible—they are the very best advocates we have.

.... SIXTEEN ....

Red Flags Over Haiti

Andrea was 35 years old, but she looked more like 65. Her right eyelid was swollen almost shut, with a glassy cataract just visible behind it. Her lip was acutely deformed and engorged, her front teeth growing horizontally from the gaping hole. The floor of her nose had collapsed, making it look as if it was broken. When I asked her for her name, she mumbled it as she stared at the ground with slumping shoulders. The terrible thought crossed my mind: this woman looks less than human.

I remembered something that Dr. Adenwalla in India had told me: "The lesson we learn from human suffering is to love, and to never, never look away." It wasn't easy to look at Andrea; in fact, all I wanted to do was to turn away. Instead I smiled. I shook her hand. I asked her questions. I tried to be as respectful as possible. I told her I wanted to know about her life. No, she had never gone to school. She never married. Never had children. Her own parents had long since passed away—she had no immediate family. She worked menial jobs, selling charcoal, carrying water. Yes, she would receive her surgery today, but it many ways it was far too late. As this woman answered my questions, she looked at the ground in shame, as her deformity was somehow her fault. Andrea's surgical scars would fade after her operation; the internal scars would always be with her. What would Andrea's story have been someone had helped her out, 30 years ago, when she needed it most? What if someone had wrapped their arms around a little girl 33 years ago, and told her she could have a free cleft operation back then?

I met Andrea in Port-Au-Prince Haiti in 2008. By this time, Smile Train had set up a presence in 75 of the poorest nations in the world. We were determined to be in every developing country with large cleft populations. We had partner hospitals in Africa, the Middle East, South Asia, China, South America, Eastern Europe. For years now, we had been flying all the way around the world to help children, when right here in our own backyard, just a two-hour flight from Florida, was the poorest country in the Western Hemisphere. In Haiti, there are an estimated 15,000 children with clefts. Going into this small country, we felt confident that we could clear up this backlog in three years.

But Haiti raised some serious problems for us. Even though this population of 8.7 million people exists right off the shores of the world's wealthiest nation, Haiti ranks 149th out of 182 countries on the United Nations Human Development Index. That's pretty close to the bottom of the economic curve. When we visited in 2008, the Haitian economy, based mostly on agriculture, was in dire straits, and its health provision was even worse. More than 8 out of every 100 children were dying before the age of 5, mostly from entirely preventable gastrointestinal diseases like diarrhea. Just below half the population was illiterate. Unemployment was at 90%. And this was before the earthquake of 2010.

When we visited, Haiti had already been wracked by natural disasters, one after the other. In 2004, two tropical storms killed more than 6,000 people. Soil erosion and deforestation caused flooding and deadly mudslides, which flattened the tin and wood homes and the inhabitants within them. In August and September of 2008, Tropical Storm Fay, Hurricane Gustave, Hurricane Hannah, and Hurricane Ike killed 331 people, according to official records, although the body count was probably much higher. More than 800,000 people were left homeless and desperately in need of aid. This latest disaster came on the heels of a food crisis and violent political unrest. The high price of fuel and the basics for sustenance—rice, flour, vegetables—left hundreds of thousands of Haitians starving in the streets.

Surgeons living and working in Haiti are few and far between, and the ones who were there were seriously overextended. As we began looking for partner hospitals in Port-Au-Prince and beyond, we ran into a major roadblock. We visited every hospital the length and breadth of the island, but we could not find a single Haitian surgeon who knew how to perform a cleft surgery. Our plan to solve the cleft problem in Haiti in three years was off to a very slow start.

My first trip to Haiti was in March of 2008, coinciding with a visit from a mission group that we were funding out of the University of Miami. I took the plane from JFK, New York, a short three hour flight. In my time at Smile Train, I've traveled to some remote and impoverished places, but nothing I'd before seen prepared me for the slums of Port Au Prince, just three hours from my home. Cite Soleil in Port Au Prince is the largest slum in the Western hemisphere, home to 300,000 men, women, and children. The name translates as Sun City, but it's one of the darkest places I've ever visited: violent crime, shootings, kidnapping, and lootings are daily occurrences here. We were advised to hire armed guards to escort us; to make sure to visit in the morning, while all the gang members were still sleeping; and to make certain we got out before they woke up.

As we drew closer to Cite Soleil that morning, the stench of rotting garbage and human waste became so intense you could taste it in the air. We began picking our way across a wasteland of excrement and trash. I had a moment's concern about my shoes, until I looked around and noticed that most of the children gathering around us were barefoot. Ahead of us were shacks made of tin scraps, wood, rusted iron, and cinder blocks. We passed a parade of people carrying plastic water containers back and forth—there's no electricity here in Cite Soleil, let alone running water. The kids kept following, chattering, smiling, and waving at us. Whenever we travel, we always look at clothes as an economic indicator. Not having shoes is bad, not having a shirt is worse. In Cite Soleil, kids were walking around completely naked. These children also had the telltale signs of malnutrition: bloated bellies, bald patches, and brittle hair with a reddish tint. We learned that the stagnant pools circling these slums were breeding grounds for dengue fever and dysentery. Suddenly I heard a horrifying snorting sound—wild pigs were foraging in the wastewater flowing around the perimeter. So many homes and lives built on a mountain of trash. No trees. No streets. No sidewalks. No relief.

Half the population of Port Au Prince is living on less than a dollar a day. Meanwhile, the price of rice keeps rising. A few weeks before our visit food riots left seven people dead. The hunger is so bad, it even has a nickname, "Clorox," because it feels like bleach eating away at your insides. During our stay, we went to the market and saw cookies made out of mud with a little bit of sugar sprinkled on top that people eat to stave off hunger. Three hours from the U.S., where obesity is one of our major health problems, people are eating cookies made of mud.

We walked around for about an hour, poking our heads inside some of the shacks that pass for homes. A few hovels were constructed out of the abandoned shells of old cars. Little shanties were made out of cinder blocks with padlocked doors and flimsy plastic roofs. There were dirt floors inside, and little furniture except for the occasional plastic lawn chair. Beds were made of wooden planks on bricks, with a thin, filth-encrusted blanket for a mattress. Amid all this sadness, we met, saw, and shook hands with dozens of children during our neighborhood walkabout. Very few were able to attend school. We showed some of the children pictures we had taken of them, and each time it drew gasps of astonishment. Most had never seen pictures of themselves, let alone a digital camera. It made it all the more horrific that stuck in the squalor were these beautiful little kids. DeLois was in tears; I was speechless.

I thought about all those news reports I'd read back home about boats of Haitians sinking off the coast of Florida. Until now, every time I read those stories, I would wonder, Why do they put so many people in the boat? Don't they know that the boat is going to sink? In Cite Soleil, I understood precisely why Haitians were leaving this slum in droves, risking their lives in small boats in the hope of making it to the U.S., or the nearby Turks and Caicos. If I were 16 years old living in Cite Soleil,

I'd settle for a plank of wood and do anything to get away.

On our way back downtown, we saw another sight that is ingrained in my memory: a red flag flying outside on of the houses. Our guide told us that a red flag is the sign of a voodoo witch doctor in residence. He also explained to us that these local witch doctors advise parents of babies with clefts that in order to cure the family of this "curse" they need to tie a rope around a child's ankle, attach it to a concrete block, and throw the baby into a sewage canal to drown. It was 100 degrees outside, but the idea of witch doctors living in broad daylight advising parents to murder their own children sent a chill down my spine.

With a certain amount relief, then, we entered the compound of the small private hospital just a few miles from Cite Soleil where the mission was being staged and where a team of doctors from Miami was going to be operating for the next three days. When we arrived, crowds of families were already waiting in the courtyard to be screened. The surgeons could only help a hundred patients in three days. It was clear that we were going to have to turn others away, with the promise that we could come back again in the very near future.

Here in the courtyard that I met Andrea, the 33-year-old woman waiting in line for a surgery. Andrea had grown up in Cite Soleil. I tried hard to imagine the degree of her suffering, living in a slum like Cite Soleil, told she was cursed and that she should be dead, unable to have any meaningful contact with the people around her, an outcast in one of the most godforsaken places on earth. I couldn't even come close.

When we flew back to New York the next day, I felt raw. The situation in Haiti rattled and depressed me more than these trips usually do. I call this feeling "the bends." The transition between such extreme poverty and day-to-day existence at home in New York is literally like changing atmospheres, and on those return flights home, we come up for oxygen way too fast. I usually shake it off this feeling of dislocation after a few days and get back into the rhythm of my work duties, but this time the intensity of the dismay stayed with me. I kept thinking about Andrea. I couldn't shake the thought of the expression on her face.

I decided to call on one of our biggest celebrity supporters to help raise more money and awareness of the cleft problem in Haiti: Christopher Meloni, of the TV series Law and Order. Maybe more people would care about these forgotten kids if Chris could bring some more attention to this cause. The reality is that in the current culture, celebrities are powerful figures, and when a celebrity decides to shine a light on a particular problem or part of the world, it's not lip service, it helps. People in the media pay attention. More people want to donate.

In February of 2009, I was back in Port-au-Prince, to escort Chris and his wife Sherman to see the work of another mission team. This time, our doctors had set up in an old Baptist mission hospital just outside of Port Au Prince, up in the hills. It was tiny, and the facilities were basic, but it had one well-maintained operating room. Beyond the hospital quarters, you could see the steep hillside, where the hospital had put in terracing to help ward off erosion. Since our last trip, workers at the hospital had been busy getting the word out across the island, distributing posters and flyers, running radio ads. Over two hundred children and adults with clefts showed up for help.

If they felt at all overwhelmed, neither Chris nor Sherman showed any outward signs of it. They plastered smiles on their faces and dove into the crowd, chatting with children and their parents. I guess show business is good training for experiences like this: you have to act as if everything is okay, keeping any expression of discomfort in check. Through an interpreter, the couple asked patients and family members how they heard about Smile Train, how far they'd come, what life was like with a cleft, and what they hoped their life would be like after the surgery. For Chris, this was a serious fact-finding mission, and he was determined to come away with answers about the impact of every dollar spent on this cause.

After an hour or so, families were getting nervous because there were so many people in line. Who was going to be helped and who would be turned away? This fear was especially intense for Bartholomew, a 42-year old man who timidly approached Chris to shake his hand and thank him. Bartholomew saw all the children registering for surgery and was certain that the youngest patients would be our first priority and he would be sent home. He had deep slits on both sides of his mouth, with teeth protruding uselessly from under his nose. He could barely speak. As with Andrea, all I could think was, "another life wasted."

Bartholomew waited in line. He was seen by the doctor. The doctor told him that they would be able to operate the next day. Bartholomew gave the doctor a look of disbelief. And then something incredible happened. He tried to argue with the doctor—let one of these children be helped instead. Bartholomew knew precisely the road ahead. But the doctor wasn't swayed. He told Bartholomew, "I'll make sure I do your surgery at the end of the day, when I'm finished with everyone else."

Bartholomew nodded and disappeared into the crowd, his hands cupped around the piece of white paper with the date of time of his appointment.

Chris continued to walk around the ward. A 7-year old girl was waiting in line, and Chris started chatting with her. Like Bartholomew, Bergaline had a double cleft lip but, thankfully, she wouldn't have to wait four decades for her surgery. Her mother told us her name was Bergaline, that no one in the family could read, but a neighbor had told her about he'd seen poster advertising the Smile Train mission. Bergaline was examined—she was in good health, and the surgery could take place that same afternoon.

Later that day, Chris offered to carry the little girl to the operating room, so he could observe a cleft surgery for himself. He helped prep her, put the anesthesia mask on her face, and watched her fall asleep.

"Make sure you give her a beautiful smile," he told her surgeon, Dr. Michael Schaefer. "She deserves the best." An hour later, Bergaline emerged from the operating room in Chris's arms. Dr. Schaefer's surgery had gone perfectly. When she saw her daughter, Bergaline's mother began jumping up and down, hugging Bergaline, hugging Chris, hugging the doctor. Tears were flowing down her face. Chris was crying, and so was I. Nearly 15 years after I saw my first cleft surgery in China, the look on the faces of these parents never fails to floor me.

That evening, Chris reaffirmed his commitment to Smile Train as a donor, but he also made it very clear that wanted to lend us his voice. He understands that his celebrity gives visibility to causes like this, and that we can attract more donors as a result. Before that day in Haiti, I think Chris thought of us simply as a well-run charity that was doing some good work and helping a lot of kids. But this trip instilled in him a much greater sense of urgency, just as it did in all of us. He'd seen two hundred people lined up outside in the hot sun, waiting their turn to register for the surgery. He knew there was no way our mission doctors could get to them all in three short days. The sight of all those desperate and disappointed families was hard to take. On our return, Smile Train made a firm commitment to fund more missions to Haiti every three months. Chris wrote a report for us about his trip that went out to more than a million of our donors. He went on TV shows to talked about us. The video he made of his trip is on YouTube, where it's been watched by thousands of people. With his help, we raised many more thousands of dollars.

Even so, despite our efforts, our progress in Haiti felt negligible. Then, after the earthquake of 2010, it ground to a halt. Life and death medical issues must take priority in Haiti right now—the doctors working there are overburdened beyond description. Since the earthquake, we've helped to support surgical teams flying in, helping with the general recovery effort, but until some kind of stability is restored, clefts will have to wait. However at some point, we will go back. Over the years, I've encountered so many adult patients like Andrea and Bartholomew. In India, a 35-year-old woman tugged at my shirt and told me, "I was never able to get married because of this." On a trip to the Kenyan border with Somalia in 2010, I met a 63-year-old woman who was only just getting her lip repaired. Surgeons have told us about adults patients as old as 85 receiving the operation. This defect can be fixed. It's unconscionable that there are in this world who go to their graves with their clefts still unrepaired.

At a small fundraising dinner after I returned from Haiti, I talked about the trip, showing a picture of Bartholomew, the older man we had met at the mission hospital in Port au Prince. One of my donors, obviously annoyed, raised his hand.

"I thought this was a children's charity!" he complained.

"Yes," I told him. "We are a children's charity, but sometimes it takes us a little time to get to the children we serve. Look closer at this picture, and you will see a two-year-old boy who has been waiting for someone to help him for 40 years."

Patients like Batholemew, waiting their turn, are the harbingers. The remind us of what's to come if we don't move fast enough to help children while they're still children, before they can grow old.

.... EPILOGUE ....

As I write this, it's fifteen years since I was sitting on that subway train in New York City looking around me and thinking, "Why aren't these kids getting helped?" In the twelve years since we founded Smile Train, I ask myself that same question every day. Why are there children suffering with clefts in the world when there's a 45 minute, inexpensive surgery to fix this problem? We just have to work harder, think smarter, and keep going, and I believe we will get to a point where we no longer have to ask that question. Period.

For some time now, we have felt that we have been making good progress toward our goal of eradicating unrepaired clefts worldwide. Thanks to a genius economist called Steve Levitt, though, we've recently figured out a way of accurately measuring our progress. Steve is the author of the best-selling book Freakonomics, and he's also a longtime Smile Train supporter and member of our board of governors.

"Why do you always say that the average age of your patients his seven years?" Steve asked me one day.

"Because that's how we measure our progress," I replied. "We're always tracking the average ages of our patients, because as the average age comes down, it shows we are clearing the backlog of clefts in the countries where we work." In the United States, where the majority of children have their surgery in the first year of life, the average age of cleft patients is less than a year and so it follows that the backlog of patients waiting for surgery is zero. When we can say that all Smile Train patients are less than one year old, then that will prove that there are no older patients left to operate on, which means we will have cleared the backlog, and that our surgeons are only operating on babies, just like in the U.S.

Steve patiently waited for me to finish my speech, then he said, "Brian, you shouldn't be looking at average age, you should be looking at the median age, the number in the middle. The average age doesn't tell you anything. The median age is harder to calculate, but it's what economists use as the truer measure."

Of course I am not a statistician, nor a genius like Steve, so I didn't know this. Right away, we reconfigured our charts, and when we saw the results we couldn't believe our eyes. Yes, the average age for our patients was about 7 years, but when we looked at the individual countries where we work, the median age was much lower. In China, for example, the median age of patients now stands at 1.7 years. In 2003, the year we started collecting digital patient charts, the median age of our patients was a much higher 4.4 years. By calculating the median age, we learned that we were reducing the backlog in China at a much faster rate than we had imagined. Today, around half the children we operate on in that nation aren't having to wait for surgery at all. This was phenomenal news! Next we looked at India. Since we started out in India seven years ago, we have brought the median age of our patients down by 50%, from 5 years to 2.5 years. Then we looked at every country in the world where we work. Almost without exception, every country in which Smile Train is performing significant numbers of surgeries, the median age of patients is plummeting.

Ever since the first cleft occurred about 200,000 years ago with the advent of modern homo sapiens, the number of clefts has grown at the same rate as the world's population. In 1341—when King Tut was born with a cleft—there were approximately 72,000 clefts in the world. When Christ was born over two thousand years ago, the number of clefts in the world had climbed to 242,000. When the

United States declared independence in 1776, the number of clefts in the world soared to approximately 1,128,000. Today, there are about 10 million children and adults in the world who have been born with clefts. The good news is that for the first time in more than 200,000 years of human history, the total number of unrepaired clefts in the world has stopped going up—and started going down. More cleft surgeries are now being performed in the world than new babies with clefts are being born.

Within five years in China, we hope to clean up the entire backlog of children waiting for cleft surgery, at which point, our surgeons will only have to operate on newborns, just like surgeons in the United States. In Chennai in India—the city where I began my travels as Smile Train's president—Dr. Jyotsna Murthy rarely sees any older patients these days, because she has cleared her backlog. Today, she is operating almost exclusively on babies and very young children. This means she can devote more and more time to passing the torch to the next generation of Smile Train surgeons in India. In 2009, a young maxillofacial surgeon called Dr. Nitin Naik won a coveted fellowship to train with Dr. Murthy in Chennai. Under the terms of the fellowship, Dr. Naik agreed that once his training was complete, he would start a cleft program in one of the smaller Indian cities, somewhere with a high concentration of unrepaired clefts. Dr. Naik chose Darjeeling, in North West Bengal, in the foothills of the Himalayas, where he has founded a Smile Train center in a tiny mission hospital, the first cleft facility in this area. Dr. Naik intends to work his way through his backlog, until like his mentor in Chennai, he is only operating on newborns. "All my life I have wanted to help others," Dr. Naik has told us. "Smile Train has made my dream come true."

Stories like this are a dream come true for me too. Twenty years ago, I had what I thought was a fantasy of a for-profit career. I made more money than I ever wished for or deserved. I got to travel on first class airplane tickets, staying in four-star hotels. But these memories have faded, replaced by the intense experiences of traveling for Smile Train, visiting refugee camps, slums, and war zones all over the globe. What I've learned on my travels is that helping children is an addiction. You help one child and the next thing you know you want to help ten children. You help one thousand children and then you want to help one million children. It gets in your blood. I know now that I will never go back to my for-profit career and for one very good reason: working for change in the world feels so much better than working just for yourself. No other job can compare to it.

As Smile Train brings more and more doctors into the fold, enabling us to help more and more children, my thoughts turn to the future. One of the hardest parts of my job has been meeting all the children on my travels that Smile Train doesn't try to help. Wherever I visit developing countries, I inevitably encounter children who have medical problems other than clefts. More often than not, I know that these are problems that can be fixed with simple surgeries and that in some cases, the intervention is even cheaper and just as effective as a surgery to mend a cleft. A child who is blind can be given a surgery that takes four minutes per eye, which allows him to see the very next day, and which costs less than $100. A child with a clubfoot can be helped with simple castings that cost $80 and that can straighten out legs in a matter of weeks. A child who is born with hole in the heart will die before the age of 18 if that hole isn't mended, but heart surgeons are hard to find in developing countries, and the surgery costs $2,000. Tragically, there is no Smile Train for these kids, and most of them do die far too young or go on to live very difficult lives. As I look to the future, I can see that this is the next step—taking the Smile Train model and applying it to other fixable medical problems afflicting children in the developing world.

It's the same question again: Why aren't these kids getting helped?

What Smile Train proves beyond a doubt is that local doctors are more than willing and capable of helping their own communities. If we just provide them with some extra resources and training, the potential is limitless. We've shown that it's possible to help very poor, but very proud communities, become self-sufficient, one smile at a time. We've also shown that it is possible to take a simple idea—empowering local doctors to do a single surgery—and to scale it up. Today, Smile Train provides 10,000 surgeries every month.

All of us at Smile Train are very proud of how far we have come, but we are also aware that we are far from finished. This is no time to rest on our laurels. A new baby with a cleft is born in the developing world every three minutes, and for the vast majority of these babies, Smile Train is their only hope. I have no doubt we will finish the job, that we will help every child who needs us, and that we will solve the 200,000 year old problem of clefts for good. When we do, no one will be smiling more than me. But until then, we have work to do, many more children to help, and miles to go before we sleep.

Onward!

.... ACKNOWLEDGMENTS ....

First and foremost, I want to thank the thousands of participating doctors, nurses, anesthesiologists, social workers, other medical professionals and non-governmental organization workers who make our programs possible. It is through the hearts and hands of these modern-day Good Samaritans that every child is helped. Over the past 11 years I have had the honor of meeting and getting to know thousands of these men and women. The following doctors are just a few whom I thank from the bottom of my heart for their help, support, and friendship: Dr. Hirji Adenwalla, Dr. Jyotsna Murthy, Dr. Mukunda Reddy, Dr. Andrew Hodges, Dr. Sarah Hodges, Dr. Shankar Man Rai, Dr. Carlos Navarro, Dr. Ken Salyer, Dr. Abraham Gebere Egziabher, Dr. Ataklitie Baraki Berhea, Dr. Sissay Befikadu, Dr. Yegeremu Kebede, Dr. Dan Poenaru, Dr. Heuric Rakotomalala, Dr. James Wade, Dr. Gorin Jovic, Dr. Asrat Mengiste, Dr. Olfat Hashimi, Dr. Keith Rose, Mansoor Chowdhury, the late Dr. Casio Raposo do Amaral and his wife Vera Adami Raposo do Amaral, Dr. Shi Bing, the late Dr. Ruyao Song who was China's first plastic surgeon, Dr. Liu Xinhua, Dr. Fan Baojun, Mr. Li Bengong, Yan Ming Fu, Dr. Liu Fulin, Dr. Li Li, Dr. Shi Jun, Dr. Wang Xing, Minister Zhang Wen Kang, MD, Dr. Vithal Lahane, Dr. Rajesh Shah, Dr. Anant Sinha,

Dr. Binita Sinha, Dr. Saurabh Kumar, Dr. Prateek Kumar, Dr. Madhukar Verma, Dr. Vijai Singh, Dr. Sanjay Agarwal, Mr. Hari Om Anand, Dr. P.K. Chhajer, Dr. Bharat Sharma, Dr. S.B. Jhawar, Dr. G.S. Kalra, Dr. Akhilesh Sharma, Arun Mathur, Dr. Subodh Singh, Dr. Krishna Kumar, Dr. Parthapratim Gupta, and Dr. N. Panchavarnam.

We recruit the best and the brightest for Smile Train's Medical Advisory Boards. These cleft experts set the highest standards for safety and quality for all our programs. It all began with the inspirational leadership from our first Medical Advisory Board chairman, the world-renowned Dr. Joseph G. McCarthy of NYU Medical Center—thank you Dr. McCarthy. Thanks are due to Dr. Eric Hubli who pioneered our surgical quality assurance program, and to the incredibly talented Dr. Court Cutting of NYU who developed our virtual surgery software and training videos with the amazing Aaron Oliker. Dr. Cutting has single-handedly done more for the education of cleft surgeons than anyone else in the world. Thanks to all the Smile Train medical advisory board members who have contributed so much of their time, energy and talent over the past eleven years: Philip Kuo-Ting Chen, Linda L. D'Antonio, David L. Dingman, Alvaro Figueroa, Ethylin Jabs, Ian Jackson, E. Heidi Jerome, Jan Lilja, Samuel Noordhoff, Judy O'Young, Brian Sommerlad, S. Anthony Wolfe, Katherine Garrett, Wang Guomin, Yongzhong, Shi Bing, Fu Yuchuan, Meng Xiang Qin, Huang Jiefu, Yan Mingfu, Zhang Wenkang, Fan Baoyun, Wang Xing, Wang Yu, Ren Minghui, Behman Daver, Mukunda Reddy, Rebecca Jacob and Karoon Agrawal.

Smile Train wouldn't exist without our donors. I want to begin by thanking our most generous donor of all, Mr. Walter Haefner. Back when Smile Train was just a good idea on a piece of paper, Mr. Haefner, agreed to give us a very large start-up grant that enabled us to start helping children immediately. Without Mr. Haefner's support, Smile Train would not be what it is today. Mr. Haefner's son Martin and Martin's wife Marianne are carrying on Walter's generous legacy, and have traveled the world to visit our partner hospitals to meet our patients and doctors. Their ongoing support has been invaluable. Over eleven years we have earned the trust of almost two million generous, wonderful, loyal donors who range in age from 6 years to 106 years old. Our donors come from all walks of life, colors, and religion. Rich and poor, young and old, liberal and conservative, Smile Train donors have one thing in common: they care about kids no one else will help. Over the years, I have been fortunate enough to meet thousands of donors. The following are just a few of these amazing individuals: Maurice Greenberg and Florence Davis of Starr Foundation, David Gelbaum and Monica Chavez Gelbaum, Ratan Tata, Ravi Kant and their colleagues at The Tata Trust, Bill and Melinda Gates, Jeff and Renee Harbers, Chuck Feeney, Bob and Mary Jane Engman, Clark Kokich and Lisa Strain, Joanne and Bill Conway, Jack Radgowski, John McDonnell and his colleagues at Patron, Nikesh Arora and his colleagues at Google, Martin Moodie and his colleagues at The Moodie Report, Ed Brennan and Lynn Arce and all of their wonderful colleagues at DFS, Olivier and Alexandra Bottrie, Dick and Pat Warren, Bob and Kathy Egbert and their daughter Emily Tabor, Linda Reeves, Harold Simmons, Betty and El Richard, Dr. Richard Bennett, Thomas Hicks, James A. Rothschild, Francine Boudewijn, Gary and Meg Krier, Victor and Cynthia Mitchell, Sir John Zochonis, Maria Pertile, Brad and Katherine Vogt, Jeff and Jane Crouth, Stan Skowronski, Larry Waterhouse, Jim Ward and his daughter Adrea Heebe, Joshua Durst, Jean Barthelemy, Bette Day, Earl and Sarah Padgett, Ann and Abigail Lurie, Marjorie Lewis, John Foord, Herbert and Svetlana Wachtell, Christopher Jeffries, Elizabeth Bynum, Elliot Jaffe, Janet Carrus, Dan Siracusa, Helena Frost, Jay and Lois Miller, Cornelia Funke, Peter Buck and the Buck Family, Carolyn Sakolsky, Tracy Chinery, Kevin MacDonald, Alistair and Sue Maughan, Lisa and John Bertani, Ralph Giannella, Evelyn Feintech, Maria Echavarria, Harold Hamm, Michael Schrader and Patricia Pierce, Harvey Chaplin, Cliff and Laurel Asness, Michele and Chad Denlinger and their beautiful son Sean, D'Ette Fowlkes, Jack Holt, Dolph Bowman, Roye and Wendy Palmer, Suzanne Bartolucci, Mike Reese, Mike and Joanne McMahon, Marshall and Mona Faith, Lillian Kimmel, Jim and Marilyn Simons, John and Gaye Iorio, Hoz Compton, Dominick Scotto, Scott Howard, Al Borgersen, Woody and Grace Dolan, Joan Tisch, Vickie and Ken French, Ann Gottlieb, Tom Cassidy, Stan Frymann, Brian and Tania Higgins, Aubrey McClendon, Greg Burke, Ravikant Varanasi, Willem Roelandts, Sergio Acle, Leo Seal, Mike Milbury, Edward Shaw, Robert Sanders, Sheila Larson, Dorothy Lemelson, Anne Smith and her team at Dubai Duty Free, Wiley Hatcher, Philip and Holly Wagner, Georgie Exarchakis and his family, the late Glenn Mustee, Ann Jones and John Coulter, Gene Montesano and Barry Perlman of Lucky Brand, Charles and Helen Dolan, John Jordan and his mother, Sally, Hall and Joan Worthington, Scott Mercer, Pierce Mangurian, Ed Ochylski, Betty Higgins, Andy Kaoh, Ruth and Roger MacFarlane, John and Lisa Stoika, Philip Niarchos, Virginia Johnston, Mike and Connie Joines, Matt and Sharon Edmonds, Peter and Wilma Veldman, Anita and Tom Veldman, Paul and Jane Helmer, Manoj Shekar, Mel and Marie Kay.

Most charities the size of Smile Train have six hundred employees. Smile Train has just 44. And it is the finest group of people I have ever had the honor to work with—they are smart, talented, incredibly hard-working, loyal and committed to a fault. Starting at the top, DeLois Greenwood, a bonafide, modern-day Saint, is the most selfless, compassionate, and dedicated person I have ever met. She has been saving kids with clefts for almost thirty years. Hard-working Hana Fuchs has been Smile Train CFO from day one and she has done an extraordinary job keeping us on track. Karen Lazarus has been my right-hand woman for 15 years and is one of Smile Train's most valuable players and integral to our success. Priscilla Ma is the genius behind all Smile Train marketing. Her talent and hard work are why we have so many committed donors today. (Special thanks also to Ron Bell and Donna Jannace who have also been instrumental in the success of our fundraising efforts, as well as Amee Kamdar, Andrew Hogue, and their genius leader Steven Levitt from Greatest Good.) The amazing Michele Sinesky has met, thanked, motivated, helped and guided tens of thousands of our donors and grass roots fundraising events. Tireless Troy Reinhart, another Smile Train veteran has been helping us from the beginning. And our hard-working, passionate and dedicated program team of Jill Woodcome, Janet Blackwood, Pam Wren, and Mackinnon Webster oversee thousands of partners and programs worldwide providing 125,000 free surgeries a year. In

Africa, Dr. Githinji Gitahi is leading our fast-growing programs with skill and devotion. In China, the indefatigable Dr. Shell Xue oversees 25,000 surgeries year with her two hardworking and talented assistants Monica and Robert. Smile Train India was built almost single-handedly by a remarkable individual named Satish Kalra. His commitment, professionalism and passion for helping children has been an inspiration and example for me since the beginning. Satish has also built an incredible team of dedicated, high-performing managers that includes Mamtaa Carrol, Dr. Ashish Sabharwal, Renu Mehta and Pooja Basu and in Bangladesh, Dr. Mahbubul Hanna. In Indonesia, one of our fastest growing regions, Simon Tobing is doing a superb job with Bernard Pasaribu and Sri Riwayati. In Latin America, the talented Francisco Flores has built our program from scratch in Mexico and in Haiti, as well as the rest of Latin America. In the Philippines, Kimmy Coseteng-Flaviano is doing extraordinarily well following the tremendous start-up success of Rogelio la O'. In Russia, Dr. Konstantin Efimov is making fantastic progress. In Vietnam, our programs are taking off thanks to Nguyen Tri Dung. In the U.K., Meg Hall does a terrific job keeping our 200,000 plus donors there happy. Other Smile Train employees, past and present who have played an important role include: Gilbert Domfeh, Amy Howard, Anna Lawrence, Shari Mason, Carlos Melendez, Buckley Milburn, Duncan Quirk, Zach Shuster, Justin Twardy, Greg Van Ullen, Amber Webb, Katie Jones, Adina Wexelberg-Clouser, Sima Zakharova, Stephen Buron, Melody Farrin, Sara Leger, Sarah Rothwell, Joy Seijas, Remi Adeseun, Som Chunharas and Ted Engelhardt. A special than you to the best plastic surgeon in Italy, Dr. Fabio Abenavoli, who founded Smile Train Italia and who has led Smile Train missions to some of the most dangerous and difficult places on the planet. Thanks to Maurits Schouten who is launching Smile Train Holland with his own money and hard work.

From the beginning, Smile Train has been blessed with extraordinary Board members who have been instrumental in our growth and success. For our first decade, our Board of Directors has been a very small, dedicated hands-on group of just seven people who have contributed to our success in many different ways. Thank you Ann Ziff, our very first chairman of the board—who has been a great friend, major Smile

Train donor, and unwavering supporter from the beginning. Rob Smits, a world-class lawyer with a big heart has been giving us wise counsel since the beginning. Mark Atkinson, a world-renowned photographer and director has been lending us his talent in a variety of ways for more than a decade.

I thank the former Vice Chairman of KPMG Tom Moser and his wife Mary Lynn who helped us launch our Board of Governors whose members include some of the smartest and most successful people in America including the famed economist Steven Levitt, Tuck School of Business at Dartmouth Professor Ken French, Avon SVP Lucien Alziari, Carlyle co-founder Bill Conway, Vice Chairman of Tata Motors, Ravi Kant, TV Star Chris Meloni, Julie Daum of Spencer Stuart, Ted Dysart of Heidrick & Struggles, Lisa Farley of UBS, and the renowned movie producer, Bradley Thomas (who traveled to Ethiopia, Kenya and Somalia with me recently.) And last but not least, the very talented Candice Bergen who has been helping us since from the very beginning. Thank you Candice for all the many things you have done for us including writing a wonderful foreword for this book.

A lot of charities actually pay celebrities to help them. We never have. Virtually every one of our celebrities have actually come on board as donors first, and then, in addition, many of them have helped us in many other ways. Thank you, then, to our celebrity supporters. The first of these were President George H.W. Bush and his wife Barbara, who helped get Smile Train off the ground. President Bush arranged a private two hour meeting with the President of China Jiang Zemin for us, and later traveled to China with Barbara to show their support for Smile Train—which is how we ended up being featured on the cover of every newspaper and magazine in that nation, not once but twice. Thank you to the late, legendary Walter Cronkite who gave us the opportunity to shoot his first Smile Train video in his historic office at CBS. Thank you to General Colin Powell, a loyal donor for years, who remarked at our ten-year anniversary at Lincoln Center, "I could have used one hundred Smile Trains when I was Secretary of State." Thanks to Tom Brokaw has been helping us from the beginning and got us on The Today Show, and to Dr. Drew Ordon flew to India to shoot a segment for his mega-hit hit show The Doctors which was seen by millions. Alex Trebek has graciously flown all over the U.S. to help host our donor thank you dinners. Jane Kaczmarek has helped us with many donor events in America and she even came all the way to India with us to see our programs firsthand. Law & Order SVU star Chris Meloni and his wife Sherman came to Haiti with us. They toured the worst slums in the western hemisphere before Chris assisted with a cleft surgery for a little seven-year-old girl. Christie Brinkley with her Cover Girl smile has been one of our best spokespeople. Thank you to Norah O'Donnell, who hosted our 10 year Anniversary Event at Lincoln Center, as well as other VIP donor events. Thanks to the famous Hollywood agent and producer Simone Sheffield, who was responsible for the movie star Aishwarya Rai Bachan coming on board as our first Smile Train Goodwill Ambassador. Ash recently shot an amazing PSA for Smile Train in which her mouth morphs into a severe cleft while she speaks. This TV commercial will be seen by millions in both India and America. I want to thank all the celebrities who have supported us financially, publicly and personally for so many years (in no particular order): Hilary Swank, Warren Buffet, Bette Midler, Robin Williams, Sir Ben Kingsley, Mariska Hargitay, Bryan Cranston, Clive Davis, Kyle Chandler, Kevin Connolly, Diane Sawyer, Helena Bonham Carter, Bob Costas, Howie Mandel, Rebecca Herbst, Senator John Glenn, Lily Tomlin, Ernie Els, Davis Love III, Rusty Wallace, Amerie, Scottie Pippen, Quimera, Daisy Fuentes, John Bishop, Donald Trump, Tom Cruise and Jeremy Roenick.

Thank you to the very talented, Academy Award winning director Megan Mylan for directing our Oscar-winning documentary Smile Pinki. Our forty-minute movie has been seen by more than 25 million people around the world and has done more to raise awareness about and help solve the 200,000 year old problem of clefts than anything or anyone.

Many personal friends helped us get Smile Train on the tracks and keep it going strong. Here are just a few that I would like to thank for their help and support: Richard and Kat Price. Kat helped launch Smile Train in China and she and Richard have been major donors ever since. The bestselling author Dr. Atul Gawande, Ralph Pascucci, his father Mike and brother Chris, Donna Winston, Chris and Laurie Raleigh, Renee

Harbers, Larry and Judy Howard, Tom Morgan, Stephen and Marnie Worth, Brad and Michelle Cuddeback, Laura Casale and her sons, Michael and Kristin Bianco, Geoff and Nora Dodge, Jeff Pagano, Cynthia Von Jako, J.P. Botindari, Ted and Sue Saraceno, John and Gretchen Mannix, George and Charlene Mclaughlin, Pat and Esther Carley, June Bremer and her daughter Annette, Suzi Schopp, Andy Pyne, John O'Brien, Ken and Gretchen Corwen, Sean and Lisa Farren, Rich VanderMass, Garth Snow, Robert DiScalfani, Caroline Firestone, Vic Levin, Mike and Wendy Darragh, Marc Sokol, Steve Rappaport and Debbie Ward. Mike Schell, my former business partner not only designed the Smile Train logo 13 years ago but virtually every ad, brochure, and important marketing piece we have done since. Mike is a very self-effacing person who rarely gets all the credit he deserves, but this time I want to make it very clear that without his talent and help support, Smile Train would never be where it is today.

Now to those people who helped to create this book you hold in your hands. After our movie Smile Pinki won the Oscar, I received a wonderful e-mail from Leslie Wells, a book editor at Hyperion. It was thanks to her encouragement, support, and brilliance that this book came into existence. Leslie helped me find a fantastic literary agent named Carol Mann, and a very talented and big-hearted writer named Eve Charles. Writing this book was one of the hardest things I have ever done but it was always a pleasure to collaborate with Eve and I am so grateful for all of the blood, sweat, and tears she put into this venture. A talented lawyer named Mark A. Merriman provided all the legal expertise for this book pro bono thanks to his boss, another genius lawyer Rick Kurnit and his renowned law firm of Frankfurt, Kurnit, Klein and Selz PC. Mr. Kurnit has been generously donating free legal services for Smile Train for more than a decade. Thanks to Ellen Archer, President of Hyperion, Kristin Kiser, associate publisher, and to Elisabeth Dyssegaard, editor in chief. Thanks to Kevin MacDonald and Navorn Johnson in preproduction, Vincent Stanley in production, Bryan Christian, Joan Lee and Mindy Stockfield in marketing, Marie Coolman in publicity, Phil Rose, art director, and to Jill Sansone, subsidiary rights director, as well as Martha Cameron, copy editor and. This extraordinary team worked to put the book together and then to send it out in the world, and am deeply grateful for their hard work and commitment to the project.

While working on this book, many months were spent interviewing dozens of people from all over the world who were kind enough to share their experiences and stories with us. Not every detail could be included, but every conversation helped bring this book to life. DeLois Greenwood, Satish Kalra, and Karen Lazarus were instrumental in this work—thank you for your patience, diligence, and insights. And thank you to everyone who shared their stories and supported our research including: Pamela Wren, Dr. Andrew Hodges and Dr. Sarah Hodges, Dr. Ahmed Nawres, Lt. Charles Duggan, Dr. Liu Xinhua, Dr. Hiji Adenwalla and his assistant Mr. Venugopalan, Miss Phyllis Treasure, Dr. Jyotsna Murthy and Christi Doss, Dr. Asrat Mengiste, Dr. Jayanto Kumar Tapadar, Dr. Joseph McCarthy, Dr. Court Cutting, Aaron Oliker, Dr. Nitin Naik, Dr. Akintububo Benedict, Mamtaa Carrol, Dr. Endale Enberber, Mark Atkinson, Dr. Carlos Navarro, Dr. Benedict Valdez, Shell Xue, Dr. Githniji Gitahi, Dr. Said Aolfat Hashimi, Dr. Youri Anastassov, Dr. Phil Metz, Dr. Keith Rose, Michele Sinesky, Melody Farrin, the Exarchakis family, Dr. Sunil Kalda, and Dr. Dan Poenaru. Thanks to Melina Moore who gave meticulous editorial support and advice and special thanks to Chris Durrance, who did as much as anyone to steer this book to completion. Thanks also to the inspirational patients and their families whose stories form the fabric of this book including: Wang Li, Pinki Kumar and her family, Xan Fu Wong, Yi Yun, Bushara and her son Mohammed, Abdulla Al Suweidy and his father Rehim, Subhodeep Mandal and his parents Sisir and Madhumita Mandal.

My own family has always been incredibly supportive starting with my parents who are amongst Smile Train's biggest donors. I want to thank my Uncle and Aunt (and Godparents) William and Arline Angell, cousins Steve Mullaney, Mark Mullaney, Ruth Angell, my mother-in-law Nan Milani, Chris and Kim Milani, John and Kim Crisp and their son Aidan, and my brothers Joe, Sean, and Evan Mullaney who have always helped and supported me.

From the very beginning, my parents instilled in all of their children the importance of service to others. I want to thank my late mother Rosemary Mullaney who always pushed me to do things I never thought I could do. Wherever she is up in heaven right now, I hope she is smiling. I want to thank my dad, Joe Mullaney Jr. who is not only one of Smile Train's biggest donors but one of our very best Ambassadors. For an annual salary of $1 he travels to major Smile Train events in places no one else will, such as Pakistan and Afghanistan, to thank and motivate our partners.

To my children Maura, Charlie and Quinn, thanks for your unwavering support and for understanding why I travel so far and so often. The best part of every trip has always been coming home to all of you. To my beautiful, patient, and supportive wife Cricket, thank you for being by my side through this great adventure, and all of the ups and downs. No matter where I go or what I do, my favorite smile in the world will always be yours.

Lastly, to all the Smile Train patients and their families, you are our heroes. Your resilience and fortitude inspire us, your struggles and triumphs humble us, your smiles and hearts lift us up. Thank you for everything you give us, every day.

Brian Mullaney
New York, 2010

.... AFTERWORD ....

As I write this, it's January 30th 2011. In a few short weeks, this manuscript will be sent off to be printed, bound, and boxed, ready to be shipped to bookstores.

Before it goes off on its journey, I want to add some news. Since finishing writing this book last October, I've begun a new chapter in my life. I've stepped down as president of Smile Train. Tomorrow, I'll be starting work at a new desk, in a new office, with a new venture.

Why would I leave the best job I ever had, working on this cause of clefts that's so near to my heart? The answer is simple: I'm ready to take the next step in the evolution of Smile Train. Since the earliest days of the organization, it's always been my dream that someday, we would reach a point where we were so well established, that we could broaden our scope. By any measure, Smile Train is in fantastic shape. For the first time since we began this work, we can say with assurance that the future of clefts is secure. Today Smile Train is one of the largest charities in America, processing 10,000 surgeries a month and raising $411,000 every single day. After twelve years and 600,000+ surgeries, we're beginning to see the finish line. Worldwide, our surgeries have peaked, and in some places, even begun to decline. With more than two million donors, the organization is financially secure too. It's clear that

Smile Train will continue on its tracks, with or without me.

We've proven beyond any doubt that the Smile Train model works. Now I want to use that same model to help solve other medical problems afflicting children all across the developing world. My new venture—called Surgery for The Poor—is devoted to children with conditions that are solvable through surgery. This time, we're focusing on children who are blind, crippled with clubfeet, deformed by burns, and dying from water on the brain and holes in the heart. Virtually everything we have learned in our mission to solve clefts, we can use to help save the lives of these children too.

I know from first hand experience that the need is immense. In the developing world, surgical procedures are a luxury that the vast majority of patients can't afford. On hundreds of trips around the world these past twelve years, I've met countless children suffering with these problems. I've had scores of doctors and partners tug at my sleeve, asking for additional money to help a child desperately in need of a burn surgery, or heart surgery, or a cataract surgery. Until now, I've always been forced to decline.

"No, I'm sorry," I'd say. "Our mission is clefts-only. That's all we can spend our donors' money on."

For so many years, I've felt certain that our single-minded focus was ultimately a benefit. Smile Train is good at clefts, because that's all we do. But every time I had to say "no," I promised myself that someday, we'd be fully established, and that I'd be able to answer, "Yes, we can help you now. We can send money and we can support you."

Saying "no" hasn't always been easy. Just last year, I was in Africa, visiting Dr. Dan Poenaru, a Romanian-born pediatric surgeon working with children with disabilities all across Kenya. Every month, Dr. Dan flies from his home base just outside Nairobi, to the Kenyan border with Somalia, to his mobile clinic at the Dadaab Refugee Camp. Dan has been working at Dadaab for over seven years now, caring for families who have fled Somalia, a country torn apart by two decades of civil war and horrifying violence. The camp was originally built as a temporary home for 90,000 Somalis. At the time of my visit, more than 300,000 refugees were living here, with thousands more arriving each week, fleeing for their lives. This is the world's largest refugee camp—one of the most destitute places you'll ever visit.

"These people cannot go back to Somalia, or they will die," Dr. Dan explained to me. "But they're not welcome in Kenya either. They have no other place to go."

As we walked around the camp, we passed hundreds and hundreds of children and their parents, each one of them begging for Dr. Dan's help. Some of the children had clefts. The vast majority of them did not.

As usual I gravitated to the cleft children. Dr. Dan introduced me to a 3-year-old old boy whose cleft had recently been repaired. The repair looked great, but I could see that there was something terribly wrong with the boy's eyes.

I asked Dan to explain.

He told me that the little boys lenses were clouded with pediatric cataracts.

"There's a surgical procedure where you take out the defective lens and put in a new synthetic one in a matter of minutes," Dan told me. "It costs about $100. Tomorrow, this boy could have twenty-twenty vision, if we had the money and resources to operate on him today. But we don't, and he will most likely never receive surgery."

Dr. Dan kept walking.

I met a ten-year-old girl sitting slumped on a bench. Her legs were hanging lifelessly from her hips, with her feet turning inwards at 90-degree angles. She stared up at me. Her mother had the same desperate look in her eyes.

I asked Dan if he was able to operate on the girl. I'd heard about an innovative new treatment for clubfoot that was inexpensive and easy to deliver. "Yes, I know about that," answered Dan, trying to maintain his calm demeanor. "But I have hundreds of names on my waiting list right now."

Another boy came over to us. He had been horribly burned after falling into an open fire. Without any access to medical help, he'd spent days in bed in agony, curled up in the fetal position. Somehow, he managed to survive, but as his skin began to heal, his chin had fused with the skin on his chest. This poor child was living with his skin stretched from the bottom of his face to the front of his body. He couldn't smile, he couldn't speak, he couldn't move his head from side to side. A plastic surgery procedure called a "release" would free up the skin so that Dr. Dan could replace it with skin grafts. The results are not pretty but the impact is transforming. Was there a charity raising money for this boy? All I could do was hope.

Next we walked passed two small children lying on blankets on the ground. Their heads were inflated grotesquely. Their eyes rolled back in heir heads. They had hydrocephalus, or water on the brain.

"These two will be dead within the month," said Dr. Dan. Again, I learned there was a simple surgery to help them. You insert a "shunt"—a small, straw-like tube—into the skull and then tunnel it under the skin to the abdominal cavity where it automatically drains the excess fluid. After about a year this problem usually goes away and the children go on to live normal lives. Dr. Dan told me these shunts cost just $30 and the surgery $300. But without funds, how could he help them? These children were going to die.

Everywhere we went people waved paper slips at the doctor. Dan told us that these were notes he had written, promising treatment.

"I'm embarrassed to say some of them are over a year old," he admitted, shaking his head in frustration.

We kept talking about clefts. Dan told us how happy he was to be part of the Smile Train venture, but it was clear that the extent of the need was far greater than clefts.

This selfless doctor took us into his little hut of an office to show us a chart with the list of 1,100 different kinds of medical problems that were afflicting his patients. He pointed out that 600 of them—more than half—could be helped immediately with inexpensive surgeries that could change their lives, even save their lives.

I could only imagine how it felt to be Dr. Dan. He was here and he was qualified to help. The children were here. Their problems were solvable. All that was missing was enough money, supplies, and support to help everyone.

I came back from Kenya sobered and inspired. Soon afterwards, I began work on this book. A year later—as I finished writing the final chapters—it became clear that my work with Smile Train was also drawing to its conclusion. At the age of 50, I knew that I wasn't getting any younger. I felt that I had one more start-up left in me and that helping doctors like Dan had to be the next step. It's early days, but I've already gathered a small team of like-minded colleagues, supporters, board members and donors who wish to join me. We're going to be using the same good ideas and strategies that have made Smile Train so successful. We're going to keep bringing these problems, this suffering, and these miracle medical interventions, to the attention of the American public and hopefully earn the support of many donors, just as we did with Smile Train.

Am I a little nervous? Yes, of course. What if this new venture fails? What if I'm too old? What if these surgeries are harder to deliver? What about all the things I don't know about these problems? Yes, as with any new venture, there's a lot of risk. But I know it's the right thing to do. Until now, there hasn't been a charity in the world focused solely on surgical disease. Not one. There are thousands focused on communicable disease—handing out pills and giving vaccinations—but nobody is delivering the simple, inexpensive surgeries that can change and save lives. That's our mission. Surgery For The Poor—the world's first charity focused solely on surgical disease in developing countries.

Tomorrow, I'll go to work at my new office on 34th street in Manhattan. Nothing fancy, just a small space with a few cubicles. We're starting out with two employees, a couple of laptops, and a thirty-nine-page business plan with a chart projecting a million surgeries a year. As usual, we're thinking big.

We have no money in the bank yet, but I'm confident that we will soon. I don't think finding partner hospitals will be a problem either. I'm already getting emails from around the world from doctors and Smile Train partners—Dr. Dan included—who have heard about this new venture. They're asking—when can we start helping them? The pressure feels intense at times. But it's also a good feeling to know that people are depending on you and need your help.

Once again, the story is beginning.

Brian Mullaney
30th January 2011
New York, New York.

If you would like to make a donation
or help Smile Train in any way, please do!

Each year, more and more children
show up at our hospitals asking for help.

You can learn more about us at www.smiletrain.org.
And feel free to call or write us too.

We would love to hear from you.

Smile Train
41 Madison Avenue, 28th Floor
New York, NY 10010
212.689.9199